Just a Thought, Too
S. L. Brown

All rights reserved.
ISBN: 978-1-732-62980-6

ACKNOWLEDGEMENTS

The first time I wrote an acknowledgement was in my first book. The idea of figuring out who to thank and to show appreciation was a bit difficult. I knew that I had to thank my parents, my wife and even my kids. I knew I would say something about my military brothers and sisters past, present and future. I would thank the proofreaders and anyone that bought the book as well. I knew that I would forget some people, omit some people (who felt they should be included), and put people in that others might not have figured would be in my acknowledgements. It is a hard thing to make everyone happy when that is the goal. Good thing for me, that is not my goal. My goal is to show my appreciation where I feel it is most genuinely deserved. It does not mean I don't appreciate others who I didn't add to this list. That being said, I will do better with this one to convey my appreciation across the board. Here we go.

With great thought I figure the best way to start this is to say thank you to anyone, everyone and all the people who have impacted my life in both positive and negative ways for my growth as a person, a human, a mentor and a motivator. I may not single you out, but I learn a lot from the people I interact with on my journey of life. Thank you.

The first person that will always be thanked by me is my mother Wanda. Mom, I hope that every day I have done enough to make all the troubles, struggles, long days, long nights and frustrations as I grew up worthwhile. I appreciate always knowing you believed in everything I could be well before I ever even thought of being something more than I had been. Every one of the things I listed built me into what I am. Your support helped polish it. I am forever grateful to have you no matter how much I don't call or visit. Thank you, mom.

My pops Robert. Pops, you have always shown me about life. I learned my street smarts watching you. Because of you, I understood that everyone deserves to be treated with respect no matter where they come from. You never met a stranger and you never were too proud to sit with someone who was struggling. You didn't always lead by example, but I know damn well you always did your best. I learned from the choices you made. I have seen both good and bad. I am a better man because of those lessons. Thank you, old man. I hope you are proud of the man you raised.

After my parents I have to thank my wife, Keziah. Hopefully she hasn't stabbed me or anything by the time you (the reader) are reading this book. While I am joking, I might be serious though. The truth is, every day I wake up to make the world better for her. OK, for real, my wife, I cannot thank you enough for standing by me and helping me evolve and grow. The day we met I knew I would marry you and I knew we would take this bumpy joy ride all the way. I want you to have the world. I cannot thank you enough, my love. Even if you stab me I still will have meant every word. Not so much after though. Just saying. For the record, stabbing is rude. Don't do that. I love you, chick.

To my sons Sean and Trae. The only job I have as a father is to help you become independent, honorable and well-adjusted men. I may not be the greatest dad in the world but what I am is proud of the men you both have become. May you both find the joy in your life and change the world only the way you can.

To my other parents Edwina, Woody, Kathy and Sheryl (RIP), I thank you for all your continued support and guidance. I believe that we are stronger by being around strong people. You all have shown me so much that I am forever grateful. The same can be said for my brothers and sisters Nai, Tramel, Amber and Terry (Hairy Sax). I may not talk to you all very often but know that what I am is a reflection of what we were as kids. I have nothing but love for you all.

If you read my first book you know the next two people are the backbone to why I chose to publish my book. Air Force MSgt Steven Auchman and Army Spc Dennis Poulin were both killed in combat in Iraq and Afghanistan respectively. My brothers, I carry on doing what I do best because you could no longer carry on doing what you wished to do. I may not have known either of you well as individuals but what you are to me as fallen comrades is unbreakable. I hope to honor both your memories as long as I live. Thank you, brothers!

Added to those two are all the men and women who serve this country honorably. Thank you isn't enough for the work, sacrifices and lives you all give for my freedoms. Be safe and get home to your loved ones.

To my hippie-witch-yogi-ball-of-energy, Beckie. I am so proud of you, kid. I know if there is a "head cheerleader" spot on the field for what I am doing you would own it. Thank you for all your support but more importantly, thank you for standing up and making a difference in the world. You've come a long way and, boy, does time change us. In this case for the better. I look forward to the future, my friend.

The last person I will individually thank is my assistant, partner in literary crime and all around do-it-all chick, April. My friend, this adventure does not happen the way it does without your drive, your belief and your many, many, many, many, many (are you twitching yet?) hours spent building what we have accomplished. I can never thank you enough for helping me bring a dream to life. I am forever grateful for you. I look forward to all the amazing adventures we will have, my friend.

I am almost done. I promise. The last group I want to thank is group of kids from South Kitsap High School, in

Port Orchard, Washington, from the 2017-2018 school year. The Reading Seminar class of 20 or so kids who were the first to use my first book *Just A Thought* as a part of their reading. You all showed me that my words have impact and that we all have a way to help others. Coming into your class and talking to you all was eye-opening, humbling and an honor. I hope each one of you recognize that your potential is only limited by you. Get out and be amazing. I saw some amazing young kids in that room. Prove to the world you belong out front.

Alright, get to the rest of the book!

INTRODUCTION

On Mother's Day of 2017, I released my book *Just A Thought* to the world. When I released it I was happy to just simply have written a book that I could give to my parents. I hoped that some of my friends would buy it because they wanted to or to just support me. What I didn't think was that anyone else would care too much about it, be interested or even take a second look. That might be a bit of being protective of myself with measured expectations, but it was what I was thinking at the time. In any case, I ordered 100 copies of the book to do author signings and events at bookstores, coffee shops and wherever people would have me. I was hopeful that my charm would, at the very least, sell a few books if not all of them. One thing I have never lacked is confidence in my ability to sell stuff. Even so, I did mean the word "hopeful" as I had never gone out this far on a limb before with anything of mine. What I knew was that it would be interesting to say the least.

A strange thing happened with the first book. It was not just good According to the feedback I started getting from readers, it was really good. I started getting messages about my book, how it touched people, made them think, made them cry and how it was just what they needed. I had people buy multiple books for friends and family. I even had one bought for a time capsule for a tiny baby named Jackson to be opened on his 21st birthday because his grandmother loved my book so much. These things were hard to understand by someone (myself) who declared, on a regular basis, mind you, that he was not a writer. These people are telling me they love my writing? Maybe I am a writer after all. Maybe there is a niche for my style of writing and my messages. Maybe I should do, can't believe I am saying it, another book. If you are reading this introduction, then you already know that another book is exactly what I decided on doing.

If you read my first book, then you know I shared my messages as they were and in order as I posted them online from May 2010 to December 2014. This second book will continue that journey as I post the remaining "thoughts" to date. I will also include my blog posts from my website, *seans-thoughts.com* as well as finishing with pictures and messages from my other social media pages. I am still shocked at all that has changed since

April (La Delfa) and I started putting book one together in January 2017. I am now a blogger and, can't believe I am saying it, a hashtagger too. One of the biggest changes is I am also a motivational speaker and conduct wellness workshops focusing on the individual. What a difference a year makes. I could go on about that but this intro is about this book or should be at least. Let's get back to the point.

This book is different from the first as I have it sectioned off in three parts. Part 1 is the continued messages from my original thoughts. Part 2 contains my blogs that my original thoughts (book one and part one) have transformed into. Part 3 will be the inspirational passages, most with pictures, I shared with friends either in private messages or on social media. These three parts make up book two. Even though it is slightly different, the goal is the same as the first book, and that is to make you think, pause, and possibly gain a new perspective on a belief or a way of thinking. As I say often, I do not want to be right or someone who knows everything. I want to be someone who helps others look a little differently at life and the world we all live in. So, without further ado, I bring you *Just A Thought, Too*!

Part 1

Continuing the Thought

Happy New Year to each and every one of you. Many people have set New Year's resolutions or "intentions" like they do every year and, unfortunately, by March most will have given up on those very goals. This year I suggest working on the one thing many people fail to see as the most important building block to being a better person. That being working on "self!" No, I am not speaking of getting skinnier, being nicer, calling friends more, being a better spouse or parent or friend, etc., etc., etc. No, I mean working on the "self" that we see in the mirror. The person that no one else gets to see except maybe a very select few. The "self" that posts "I don't care about (insert topic)" and then spends the night crying about it. The "self" that takes back the husband, wife, boyfriend, girlfriend that does nothing for them because being alone is scary. The "self" that feels it can't be true because people will judge it and friendships will be lost. The "self" that drives us to hate, to reach out for negative and give it back to the world or to give our bodies away to those who don't deserve to even look at us, let alone have sex with us. The "self" that makes us share Facebook memes talking about how bad we are at self-love, self-worth and the like, posting "I am so #4 and #6 on this list" in hopes that this proclamation will make us feel better. The "self" that requires us to say "so beautiful" or "pretty" or "bella" (for my Spanish friends... I think, lol) to every picture someone posts even when it doesn't warrant it. This is the "self" that people who are genuinely happy have worked on, have built up, have invested in and have nurtured for strength and resolve.

One of the biggest fallacies of our time is that we can love others more than ourselves. We cannot! In order to truly love as we are able to do we must love ourselves authentically. We must look to better ourselves not out of loathing what needs to be changed but out of loving yourself enough to change. To lose weight with love means every pound is a success, every day you make it to the gym and burn those calories is a success, every time you choose an apple over candy is a success. Then it becomes something you WANT to do and not HAVE to do.

As you embark on your journey of 2015 take the time to get to know your "self" and understand the hurts, the pains, the joys and amazingness that is "you!" It is time to be better people... You in? Just a thought, friends. (Note: If you read this far I challenge you to share something you love about yourself. If you don't it is all good I appreciate you anyway. I'll even go first)

My response to the challenge: One thing I love and appreciate about myself is that, no matter how I feel, be it up or down, I can bring a smile to a friend's face. It always brightens my mood. Being able to bring a smile or laugh is a gift I cherish in me.

Jan 5, 2015

*****

What if we knew the day, the moment, the exact second we were going to die? What if that day was today? I often think to myself, "If I died what would people remember of me?" I wake up every morning and the first thing I do is make my wife smile and then I send out "good morning" messages to a few friends to make them smile. I don't do this to feel good about myself but to remind a certain few that life is shorter than we think and in it we have only one go around. So live, love and laugh for no reason at all." Every day someone dies having a heart full of regret for things never said, never done and never imagined. This isn't a YOLO (you only live once) type thing but a Live Every Tiny Moment Exceptionally (LETME.... yup, I just made that up.) thing.

Let today be the day you start to heal those wounds of anger and hate. Let today be the day you share a smile and a positive action rather than a frown and a negative one. Let today be the day you "Pay It Forward" no matter how small or large the gesture, be it sharing a great photo, calling an old friend, messaging someone, commenting on a stranger's great shirt, pretty eyes or awesomeness in general. If you only had one more day, hour, minute to live would you waste it on hating the person in the mirror? LETME act like today may be the last so I can enjoy tomorrow that much more. What say you, friends? It's just a thought!

Jan 15, 2015

*****

Want to take a minute to remember Dr. King. Every man or woman is flawed and has their own demons to bear. However, in spite of that, some stand up and try to lead for the greater good of ALL instead of the greater good of SELF. I am ashamed to be a part of a society that seems to be heading in the wrong direction of equality for all. What did Dr. King and those who fought for freedom and equality (not just Black rights but women's rights, gay rights, etc., etc., etc.) give their lives and energy for after all? Every few months we have a "war" on something or someone. At present it is against the police. Let me sidetrack for a minute. I am sick of people being racist and calling the police racist. Yes, it is the same damn thing! To say all White cops are racist is, in fact, being racist. There are good cops and bad cops and each (NOTE: EACH) situation is its own situation that should be looked at in that fashion. Instead of filling my Facebook page with hate clips, why don't people get off their respective asses, put down the weed and alcohol, and join the police force to protect their own neighborhoods. I mean this for ALL races and cultures. Dr. King fought for the right for people to be able to be police officers because they had the skills to do it. He fought for the right for women to be high level managers and owners who got equal pay for their talents, not because they had a nice rack and great butt.

OK, another rant: I am also sick of seeing women complain about not being taken seriously or getting equal treatment while pulling out the "mom" card or dressing like they are going to the club. There is a difference between tasteful and tasteless. That doesn't mean women need to dress like Amish people but don't get mad that others are looking, commenting or being judgmental of the blouse or top that barely covers her nipples. And yes, being a mom is hard but so is being a dad and so is being childless. Equality means there are no special considerations to anyone for anything. If one gets it then all get it.

Dr. King fought for equality for us all to RISE to the standards set by those who already had something. He didn't want education to be lowered so others can feel better but instead wanted others to be able to rise to those educational standards. Unfortunately today, we fight for the right to write papers in Twitter speak, for our young girls to dress like strippers at school, to get high on weed (because we can't take the pressure), to be able to put minimum effort (C student) into higher education and get a degree for free, to receive all those medications (that we don't need) for free, to work a low-skill job for high-skill pay and/or to be a victim who is not accountable for our own actions. Yes, we fight for those things as people of America. Dr. King had a dream and died setting it in motion...sadly, someone pushed that train onto a different track and it is going out of control the wrong way. It is time to evaluate ourselves not as Black people, not as White people, not as Hispanic, Latin, Asian and all other racial titles, but as human beings. The greatness of Dr. King's dream is that a dream, even if dead, can't be killed. We can revive the ideals of it and stop the idiots from speaking for all of us and start lifting each other up to be better. It is time to raise the standards for all of our people...Just a thought!

Jan 19, 2015

*****

Monday found me traveling to another class;

Thoughts of the day ahead as the world passed;

And as car after car passed through my gaze;

I wondered how would Monday treat me in a bad way;

Then I looked up and took a deep breath deep inside;

And as I exhaled I began to see the wonders of my drive;

I pass a cove with tiny waves as the sun crest the sky;

And way in the distance I see the snow-capped mountains standing high;

Just like that my Monday had become better and smile crept on my face;

Then I saw a view and to my friends I couldn't let it waste;

So here is your case of the Mondays from the Great Northwest;

Now, what will you give to the world to make this Monday the best?

Jan 26, 2015

*****

As I finish final preparations for my very first "OMG this is my, for real, my name is on the schedule" class (tonight Bremerton Family YMCA at 1730), I am left to reflect on what that really means to me. In my life I have been told both directly and indirectly that I couldn't do something, don't fit the bill, can't get to "that" point and a million other versions of that type of doubt. Luckily for me, I could care less what others believe I "can't" do and instead I surround myself with people who say go ahead and do it, you got this, why the hell not, OK let's go, etc., etc., etc. You see, I don't get to where I am without first believing in myself. I don't stand on a mountain being carried. I stand on it having climbed it. My parents, spouse and kids have helped me to gain that strength to carry on when I have not had the energy. And for that, I am forever grateful.

I also have non-related supporters who don't simply cheer me on but help to guide me when I need it and to them I am grateful. That all being said, today I am grateful for my lil Terror Lupita (Fitness 19) who always pushed me to get my Zumba Certification and all the hours she spent answering my questions and mentoring me. I am thankful to the instructors who allowed me to lead in their classes and pushed me to the front like Laura (Fitness 19), Bremerton YMCA Staff and Instructors and lil Ms. Deb (YMCA). These instructors greeted me with open arms and helped to grow my passion further. There are a bunch of other people and instructors I can thank for helping me to this first milestone of my teaching. Just know if you are reading this...THANK YOU! Today, I start a new journey. It is time to see where this road will take me.

Feb 03, 2015

*****

If you know me personally then you know I pretty much hate Valentine's Day. It always seemed to me like those churches you go to where it seems more fashion show than about the Word of God. It became a day to show off "my man is better than yours." Of course, very few people will admit that but the actions speak volumes. If you are in a relationship, shouldn't every day be Valentine's Day? Shouldn't we always want to remind our mate (hell, even our friends) how special they are to us? Yes, I hate the day, but I love the intent behind it. So, to all my wonderful friends, both in a relationship or not in one, I wish you the best day that makes you smile and feel valued. Then, I wish you to be able to give twice as much to someone else. My wife Keziah is always my Valentine. Now the rest of you can be too. :) May we all find simple enjoyment in the things we don't have to have to compete against the world. How was your Valentine's Day?

Feb 14, 2015

*****

The inventory of one's life will not be taken in how many items he or she has attained. It will not be in the number of men or women that have been bedded. It will not be in the piles of cash accumulated over the years. It will not be in the number of mini-me's brought into the world. It will be on how the gift of life has been cherished. It will be on how one has treated his or her mind, body, spirit and soul. It will be how he or she has lived in authenticity to himself or herself. It will be in how many smiles attained. In the number of men and women helped out of a spiral of darkness. It will be in the piles of friendships and goodwill accumulated in the memories of others. It will be in the reflection of self-worth, self-respect, self-reliance that was given to those previously mentioned "mini-me's" and how he, she, or they carry it on. When it is time to go, what will your inventory sheet look like? Just a thought, my friends!

Feb 26, 2015

*****

If you don't believe in you, your dream and your ability to get it done... why should anyone else? People support you, people back you, people advise you, people cheer you on but the first and most important person in a chain of success is "You." If others squelch your dream, then you didn't really believe in it in the first place. You don't need self-help books, positive proclamations and memes or a rah-rah crew to believe in your journey. All you need is faith that every hurdle and step backwards is a lesson and every triumph is a new victory. Be the loudest, biggest and most dedicated supporter of your journey. Then, and only then, bring along some great people to share the journey with you. You ready to make it? Just a thought, friends!

March 05, 2015

*****

Remember every darkness has a light and every rainstorm gives way to the sunshine. Life isn't easy because an easy life does not build you up. Instead, it sets you to fall further when, not if, hard times come. The measure of a person cannot be determined in the things that he or she can smile about but by the resolve to smile, hold faith, keep the course, stand strong and be the values that he or she lives by in the darkest of times be it religious conviction, personal conviction or some other form of standard he or she lives by. We all have times when we want to raise our hands and simply quit, go build a tent out of pillows and pretend the world no longer exists, but the strong stand up, wipe the tears, shake off the frustration, look life in the face and say, "You won't break me!" This message is for all who are going through something and they just can't see an end to the crap in their life. Remember things can be replaced, steps backwards aren't a "surrender" but instead it's "readjusting." No man, woman, financial woe, physical ailment or other struggle is strong enough, dark enough or hard enough to break or beat the spirit we all possess within us. So, pray to your God, meditate to your Deity, stand with your loved ones, stand on your own or whatever it is that "YOU" do and hold value in and GET UP! Dark days don't define you. They build you. Today choose to be built stronger, better, wiser and more determined than ever before because you got this... Just a thought, my friends!

March 25, 2015

*****

As I sit and think about the Airman (MSgt Auchman-Iraq 2004) and the Soldier (Spc Poulin-Afghanistan 2011) that died in combat, I have to take a moment to think about a much more tragic loss of military life. Many that know me have heard me say that war does not just affect you but it changes you to the core so much so that you will never forget its sights, sounds, smells and feelings. The glory of victory and the pain of defeat are as fresh today as they were on the day they were planted in the mind. Anyone who has been in combat knows this to be true. No matter how much we joke, how much we wish to go back (yes, a lot of us wish to go back), or how much we act like it was nothing, the truth is we are deeply affected. The loss of life of a man or woman to combat is a hard pill to swallow. The loss of a teammate rocks the unit even when every member must carry on. Having to carry the flag draped coffin onto a plane to send them to a husband, wife, parents, grandparents, brothers, sisters, and/or children or grandchildren can never be forgotten by those who survived. It is the burden we carry to our grave. That being said, the most tragic loss of military life is the current epidemic of suicide. A man or woman that wrote a check to give his or her life decides to take it instead of fighting on.

So, this thought is for my brothers and sisters in arms who can't quiet the demons of war, can't stop the dreams, can't un-see the images of teammates bloodied and battered, can't un-hear the screech of a wife or a mother as she is handed that folded flag by the Honor Guard as her loved one is put to rest. This is to remind us that the mental fatigue of serving is a real and unforgiving beast that cannot and will not be calmed by ignoring it. We did not sign on the dotted line just to stop fighting for ourselves, for our families and for each other when it seems hopeless. Today, I remember MSgt Auchman and Spc Poulin, but I also take a moment to remember all those who couldn't take the pain anymore and left the team the worst way possible. We are brothers and sisters and it is time we remember to Check 6 for each other. Just a thought, my friends.

March 31, 2015

*****

First, Happy Easter to each and every one of my friends and their families. May you sit with those you love and love those you sit with. As many will reflect on the great sacrifice and resurrection of the Son of God I am left to reflect on the "flock" that has been left. It has become a custom of both believers and non-believers to spend more time spewing hate about the other side and less time spreading the word and mission of their own faith. Did Jesus really sacrifice for that? Did he answer for the sins of humankind just to have him reflected in words and actions of hate? It doesn't matter how many pictures you post of Jesus and type "Amen", it doesn't matter how many crosses and rosaries you have on display, it doesn't matter how many verses and scriptures you can recite at the drop of a hat if you do not SHOW what it is to be within YOUR GOD's image. I may not know a lot but one thing I have come to understand is that a person can only fake it so long around other people before that person's true "self" comes out and is known. That is with people. If Biblical teachings are true, then "faking it" isn't something one can do in the presence of God.

So, as we celebrate Easter I hope we can all take a minute to ask ourselves, "What do I represent in my actions and my words?" Then ask, "If a person did not know me and only saw what I wrote and heard only what I have said, how would they view me, and does it reflect the beliefs that I say mean so much to me?" Easter is the best time to reflect on who we all are and more importantly who we wish to be as representations of who and what we believe in. This Easter may you find the mirror that looks to your soul and speaks out in a way that helps you

become a better person, a wiser person, a reflective person, an honest person and person worthy of a place next to whichever Deity you believe in. May you all be blessed! Happy Easter, my friends. It's just a thought!
April 4, 2015

*****

If Today was yesterday what would you have done differently? What would you have finished? Started? Enjoyed? Today slips by without pause, one measured moment, at a time until each has vanished forever. Today is the now! It is the moment we have and the only one we are for sure to be able to enjoy. What will you make of Today? Spend less time looking at Yesterday wondering what could have been and only a little time looking at Tomorrow considering what could be. And, instead, invest in Today and simply BE. BE amazing, BE humble, BE grateful, BE the you who you always wanted to be and, most of all, BE the light that someone else may need. LETME! Just a thought, my friends. BE WONDERFUL!
April 19, 2015

*****

To experience life fully one must fully be aware that life is a gift. It is the one thing created that we, as a species, barely understand yet walk in it every second of every day. One must feel the lows to know the greatness of the highs. One must cry in order to believe in the healing powers of a laugh. One must walk through heartbreak to learn that the heart cannot be broken. One must experience the sadness and loss of death to truly embrace the delicacy of life. We experience the bad in order to live in the good. Do you spend your days complaining, hating others and/or yourself, wishing for something else, hoping for the next big thing while trampling on the current thing you are working through?

Today, take a moment to think how much you really cherish your life. Think about how you portray it to those who don't "know" you. Would they think you were happy, sad, angry, hurt, hiding, loving, spiteful, hateful, etc., etc., etc.? Think about how those around you reflect you. Are you surrounded by love, drama, laughter, crying, spiritualism, destructiveness, etc., etc.? Our lives are a gift that cannot and should not be left in a box, put on the shelf, and stored for a rainy day. It should be embraced, played with, enjoyed, shown off, shared until it is all used up and we move on to the next life. May you take a minute this Sunday to reflect on what makes your life great and begin to experience those moments much more fully. Just a thought, my friends!

April 26, 2015

*****

I am an American! My color is black, well technically I am more caramel, but I am an American. My wife is an American! Her color is white, technically pasty or ghostly or red (sunshine time), but she is an American. My sons are American! One is my complexion and the other is light gold, I guess, but they are American. To be American isn't a color. It isn't a social status. It isn't specified by a certain heritage or a certain upbringing. It isn't a job title or held for specific groups. WE, yes, you and I, that were born in this country (or military bases around the world), are Americans. There is not a White America, Black America, Asian America, Mexican America, Goth

America, Rebel America, Tattooed America, Christian America, Buddhist America, Muslim America, Atheist America or anything else. It is just America. It is time we stop pretending that "those people" belong to someone else and that we don't know them. We are brothers and sisters of different shades, different experiences, different views on various things but we are brothers and sisters. If we really want to heal America then we, as Americans, need to start to look at how we, as individuals, are making it sick. Are you spreading hate be it directly or indirectly? Do you share images and videos that not only make you look bad but others? Are you saying one thing and then showing another? For instance, are you a woman who demands respect but then "shares" a meme talking about "Yes, we bitches but we are bad bitches!" Or a parent who thinks that their children acting out is something the world should see as a joke and then complain about how your kid doesn't listen to you?

This is not someone else's country. It is OURS and WE ARE THE PROBLEM! It is time to look in the mirror and say, "What have I done?" It is time because you are

American. Let's peel back these stupid labels and remove the GMO (Get Mine Only) from our focus and start rebuilding our community of being American across the board. Just a thought.

May 05, 2015

*****

Tomorrow we celebrate the women who carried us and protected us inside them until it was time to bring each of us into the world. We celebrate the sacrifices, the tears, the joys, the sadness, the ups and downs for the woman who could look past our faults and see the diamond even when no one else could, even ourselves. We celebrate the countless hours teaching respect, ownership, discipline, love, trust and a billion other life lessons. We celebrate the woman who watches her son leave for the military saying it's going to be alright even though she is terrified inside. We celebrate the woman who teaches her kids to be independent of her rather than dependent on her because she knows one day she will be gone and her greatest gift she could give her kids is independence.

Mother's Day, for me at least, is for those women who put one foot forward to teach their kids how to survive and excel in a world that is in turmoil. It is for those women who tirelessly work in order to see their kids have the best start for when they move into their own adult lives. I have always believed the truest testament to a parent is how the child lives as an adult, how the child respects her (and other women, especially if the child is a boy) and how much the child shows the appreciation to her.

Tomorrow, I will thank my three mothers: Wanda (#1 mom), Edwina (#2 Step-mom) and Kathy (#3 Mom-in-law) for always loving me beyond my faults but not excusing me for screwing up. I will thank them for being the voice of reason when I needed a sounding board and not judging me or getting mad if I chose a different route. Most of all I'll thank them for simply expecting me to be the man I am and pushing me to be an even better man in the future.

I'll also thank the two women who raise my boys. I can never say enough about the man Sean Jr. has turned out to be because of his mother and for that I am grateful.

Then there is my wife Keziah who has raised a young man that continues to make us proud each day with his intelligence, his compassion and his drive to take on the world. I am forever grateful for her and all that she has done.

Lastly, to all the mothers, both good and bad, who have crossed my path, I wish you all a Happy Mother's Day and hope that you feel all the love that you have given to your babies. Happy Mother's Day, world!

May 9, 2015

*****

People seem to think Freedom of (Insert speech, bear arms, assembly, etc., etc.) means to do and say whatever they want. So, I am going to use my freedom of speech to make something perfectly clear. The freedoms that we Americans are so effortlessly abusing to support our own selfish causes have been paid for by those who serve it. Lately, I have seen many pictures of people standing on or burning the Flag of the United States in some form of protest. We are AMERICA and that Flag represents us ALL. When you disrespect it you are disrespecting every man, woman and family that has served in the Armed

Forces and Coast Guard. Most importantly you are disrespecting yourself! We have built a generation and a society that believes that they are not part of the problem if they simply sit back and bitch about it. America is OUR country and it is OUR responsibility to remember that those Stars and Stripes stand for the beliefs of freedom and unity. Acting as if it is something different only separates and segregates our country more be it racially, sexually, socially, economically or religiously. We make this country. We are responsible for the high crime rates. We are responsible for the abuses of power and authority in our government and police forces. We are responsible for the destruction of our lands from unethical abuse. We are responsible for our children being on every drug possible and having no idea what respect, responsibility or ownership means. We are responsible for the morons who are home grown terrorists that would attack innocent people. It isn't America. It is WE THE PEOPLE. It is time to stop this nonsense of irresponsibility and start taking ownership of this country...or OUR country.

Final point, if you are a friend of mine and you have a picture of you desecrating the American Flag I will not go all angry. I will just remove you from my world. We will never be friends again. The same goes for people who "like" such images. Disrespecting of the many people who died defending the ideals of this nation will never be acceptable in my world and it shouldn't be in yours either. This is tragic and a pitiful example of being an American. It's time to stand up and pledge to BE AMERICAN! I know I am. Just a thought, friends.

May 21, 2015

*****

I've seen a lot of memes that express the difference between Memorial Day and Veterans Day. It has been said that Memorial Day isn't about BBQ's nor is it a celebration to praise a veteran or say Happy Memorial Day. In this I agree and disagree. Memorial Day is for the men and women who have paid the ultimate sacrifices in defending this country, from the Civil War to our current conflicts all over the world. It is a solemn duty to pay homage for the lives that could no longer enjoy the freedoms that many of us take for granted. That IS

Memorial Day! It is also about the veterans that live on because without them the fallen will be nothing more than names on a wall, a plaque or a sheet of paper, etc. Without the men and women of the 5th Air Support Operations Squadron, you, the reader, would not know the name MSgt Steve Auchman who was killed in a rocket attack in Mosul, Iraq in 2004. He lives on and his sacrifice lives on because we will not let him become another name. Without the men and women of PRT Kunar and the 181st Infantry Division you wouldn't know Spc Dennis Poulin who died in a rollover accident in Kunar Province, Afghanistan in 2011.

Every fallen man and woman has a unit and a team that will not forget their brother and sister in arms. We, the remaining few, will raise our glasses and toast the ones that cannot drink with us. We will fire up the grill and share in laughter and brother- and sister-hood for those whose eyes closed in lands far from home. You see the BBQ's and the celebrations of those who remain are just as important to the memory because it is our time to do just that, remember. So, I won't be upset if you say Happy Memorial Day because I am happy to be able to spend the day remembering all the men and women who died for me and you. I won't be upset if you thank a vet for his or her service because those who are serving and have served wrote the very same check that said, "up to and including my life." Ours just was not cashed.

On Monday another Soldier, Sailor, Marine or Airman will die in a foreign country surrounded by their adopted family of brothers and sisters which will make Memorial Day have greater meaning for all those around him or her. Let us not forget those who have gone and those who are risking it all for our freedom! To all my Brothers and Sisters in Arms: Thank You for carrying on the memory, the legacy and the honor of our fallen. See you on the other side!

May 24, 2015

*****

I have been fortunate to be raised by a father who was flawed. A father who used the belt (a lil to often if you ask my butt) and used his words. A father who fell to substances and found his way back. A father who, through everything he did, right or wrong, always reminded me to take care of my mother. A father who could not always follow his own advice but gave some of the best wisdom for life anyone could hope to receive. I don't judge my father by what I think he should have done to make my life better. I judge him on what I HAVE DONE to make my life better. Forty years have passed and I still pass on his wisdom. I know how to make people feel good about themselves because I watched him change someone's frown into a smile without any great effort over and over and over again. From the days of being called Little Slickman at the Chosen Few Motorcycle Club to being called Puffy now, I am a reflection of my father, my grandfathers and the rest of the men in my lineage. I carry my name with pride because, even flawed, my father told me it and my word were all I have to most people. And now I am a father to an 18-year-old Junior who lives with his mother and is raised by his stepdad (who is also his father). Sean Jr. carries himself, his image and his name with great pride. Then there is my 14-year-old stepson who carries his father's name, Simpson, with great pride because his mom and I make sure of it. His father and stepmom also push him for greatness. I am grateful to see both my boys grow to be great young men who I hope will be twice the dad I have ever been. To all the fathers out there I say, Happy Father's Day! Your job is to raise children who become self-sufficient adults who don't need to rely on you but know they can come to you if they really need it. Thank you to you all. (Note: Dad's don't die. They live on in your actions and the pride you have to stand on your own two feet.)

June 21, 2015

*****

Oh boy! There has been so much hate on Facebook these past few weeks that I just sat back and shook my head in disappointment. Educated people standing so strongly in what they believe that they don't see that they, themselves, are doing exactly what they are accusing others of doing. I am not going to go into all the specific things--- marriage equality, Confederate Flag, police brutality, immigration, gun rights, all things Obama and nothing Republican, etc., etc., etc. What I will do is ask this, if you stand on one side of the issue so firmly, are you really seeing the big picture or just being closed-minded? Watching people use the Constitution and the

Bible as weapons of SELECTIVE choice pretty much sickens me.

First, the Constitution was written by our forefathers for the people which did not include a lot of people outside of Whites of European decent. It did not include any people of color, women past that of their husband's wishes or other Whites from non-affluent countries. It was made to separate the church and the state...SEPARATE!

As lessons were learned, then came AMENDMENTS, which were changes to the Constitution that no longer worked for society. I am kind of partial to the 13th Amendment as I know a lot of women really enjoyed that 19th. We have the right by our Constitution but we also have the obligation to look at what does not fit for our society. The individual must also give way to the group in order for us to move forward.

I believe 100% in 2nd Amendment. I do not believe some idiot should be able to carry a fucking machine gun into Disneyland and go on It's a Small World because he has the right to do so. There is a line that has to be drawn by those who support it most to govern themselves. As long as we are no longer trying to live alongside our brothers and sisters who do not believe what we believe, see what we see, understand what we understand or feel what we feel, then we will never be what our country was supposed to be, "a place free of persecution and hate."

I don't have to agree with homosexuality to understand that the individual deserves equal treatment to what I get. I don't have to like guns to understand that the individual has a right to protect his or her home and a right to be able to responsibly buy and use (in appropriate places) all sorts of crazy guns. I don't have to believe in God to respect individuals' rights to be able to practice their religion in their homes, in their places of worship or in their society. I do have to understand what my beliefs are and how I can live them without FORCING them onto someone else in society. I can be a smoker but, if I walk down the street smoking and blowing my toxic shit into the air for others to walk in, then I am an asshole. That isn't about being a citizen but caring only about me.

That is our problem. It isn't about WE THE PEOPLE. It is about ME THE PERSON for most people. Nearly every religion that I have had the privilege of learning about has one core value... LOVE. It all starts with love. Maybe we should try doing a little more of that instead of pulling out our guns and saying, "My way is the only way!" So much hate... What a waste of the precious hours that your Gods gave you. It is time to get a rag and clean off some mirrors because a lot of us aren't looking clearly at ourselves through our own words and actions. It is time! Just a thought, friends!

June 29, 2015

*****

I don't have PTSD. Many who truly know me would say I have one of the strongest minds and spirits they have ever seen. I don't have PTSD. Life's situations don't make me crumble or fluster me to the point I either snap or shut down. They are just problems to be solved. I don't have PTSD. I have been deployed many times to foreign countries where my life was on the line. It didn't bother me then and it doesn't now. I don't have PTSD. I spent 5 months in Iraq getting bombed on an average 3 times a day (6 rockets minimum) with no shelter and, though at times I did jump and give the "Fuck, that was close," it didn't really bother me. I don't have PTSD. I spent 9 months in Afghanistan, stood in formation to watch 40+ fallen heroes get carried onto the back of a C-17 headed home and even carried one of my own onto a Medical C-130 so that he could die with his family. I don't have PTSD. I spent 9 months fighting for my family (Deployments can kill marriages.), being depended on by my unit as I was the only one not with them in Kunar and worked every day while deployed except for 14 when I went on Rest and Recover. I don't have PTSD.

So, what is this about? I can't take a nap. No, if I fall asleep unexpectedly on the couch I'll wake up defensive. I'll wake up not knowing where I am and, as war vets are prone to do, assess my situation which takes a minute or two to figure out. I must go through a mental checklist to make sure I know what the reality of my situation is at that time. I don't have PTSD. When I sleep, and my wife wakes to go to work and is getting ready to leave, she has to say my name from 5 feet or so away because if she gets to close I may wake up in defensive mode which means I am ready to attack whatever the threat is above me. Luckily, I am able to open my eyes and assess my surroundings before acting. I don't have PTSD. I hardly watch war movies that depict real life military lifestyle because it reminds me of so many things we don't talk about, both good and bad, which sometimes hurts. I don't have PTSD. I also wish sometimes I was back in a warzone where it all seems familiar and easy to me. Yes, I, like many of my fellow vets, miss the brother- and sisterhood of deployment. I even miss those rockets hitting and that whistle sound of shrapnel whizzing by our heads, buildings and vehicles because sometimes the silence of being home is crushing. Sometimes the idea of trying to be the husband or wife to your spouse and/or father or mother to your kids seems like something you may never be able to do right again. I don't have PTSD. These are just some of the things that go through a war veteran's mind. Imagine what the men and women with PTSD MUST BE going through.

Twenty-two veteran suicides a day! TWENTY-TWO men and women who sacrificed the simple enjoyment of freedom by giving their mind, spirit and body to defend it knowing they would never be the same took their lives. They have PTSD. So, this Fourth of July remember that we fly our flag (The AMERICAN ONE) in honor of those who still fight a never-ending battle for freedom. Those who heard so many explosions and have seen so much death that fireworks send them into a closet with a heart racing, sweat pouring and a mind full of painful memories.

As Americans it is time we remember the price some pay for our independence. To each and every one of the men and women who honorably wear and have worn the uniforms of this nation, I say, this 4th of July is for you. May we all be lucky enough to thank a person who took on war demons and keeps them deep within so they don't harm our loved ones. It is also time to talk about what is going on because ONE VETERAN SUICIDE IS TOO FUCKING MANY! PTSD is not the end of the world, but it can be unbearable if we don't help each other stay strong. Let's Stay Strong for Each Other! Just a thought, friends.

July 03, 2015

*****

Wow, I can chime in on a lot of things that are going on in our country but the one that is bothering me most is the war on law enforcement. First, there are bad police officers who abuse their power, who are racist (not just the White guys either), sexist and just plain not worthy of the uniform of a peace officer. Now that being said, to call ALL White police officers racist is, in fact, being racist. It amazes me how often people will complain about one thing and then do the exact same thing that is being complained about. Hypocrisy seems to be the only thing we are consistent at these days. We don't want to fix a problem. We simply want to be victims of it.

I have yet to see anyone (or very few, that is) come up with solutions to the issues at hand. Tell someone why aren't more people joining the police force, becoming litigators and bringing more positive changes to our communities (Black, White and in-between). The response is usually various bullshit about it being too corrupt. No, cowards hide behind crowds and use bully tactics to make statements without any fear of ramifications. What happens when idiots go out and kill police officers? The government sends in the military to restore order. Are we going to start shooting those soldiers? Think about that for a second.

As we run around with all these "support the troops" stickers and wristbands. Think about what it means to stand up and go towards the chaos while everyone else runs. Somehow the criminal became the thing we fight for so much that we risk our lives for it. Amazing!

I stand by innocent civilians who are victims of police brutality. I stand by protesters that mean to bring light to issues and work to find solutions to the common problems of the communities. I stand by the men and women of the police force who go out to enforce the laws of our land with no idea who is looking to kill them simply for how they are dressed and the job they perform. I stand by those in the communities who look at drugs, gangs and crime and say, "Enough is enough. I need to do something about it!" To my brothers and sisters in law enforcement, I stand WITH you. It's time to silence the idiots and take our sanity back. Just a thought, my friends.

Sept 06, 2015

*****

I have thought a lot today about what this day means to me. If you have been my friend long enough then you have seen me recap getting the "Sean, are you alright?" wake up call from my mother followed by turning on the TV to see the 2nd plane hit. If you have paid attention, you know that I cherish every life lost that day and all the men and women who have died fighting in wars ever since. That will never change.

In me, they are not forgotten. Just like Pearl Harbor, the memory is permanent in my brain and soul. To everyone still fighting... thank you! That's the part most will like to read.

Now to the rest of my point. The old saying "one rotten apple can spoil the bunch" keeps popping into my head today. Every time I remember those planes hitting the building and think of Al Qaeda taking credit, I think of that statement. What Bin Laden and company succeeded at doing was dividing our nation. Al Qaeda made "Muslim" the new N-word of the world. Saddam gained his power in part by making all the Iraqis' troubles the result of the Western world. He made Christian a bad word. He made White and Caucasian (especially American) the face of the oppressors of their nation and it worked. He played to their ignorance and we, as Americans, got played the same way. This is no different than so many Blacks today forgetting how many Whites marched and supported the freedom of the slaves. It is no different than the media showing nothing but riots in Baltimore even though there were hundreds and hundreds of peaceful protests (with all races). It is no different than a myriad of other examples. 9/11 gave us a new enemy but it wasn't the zealots that are terrorizing the countries, killing women and turning children into child warriors. No, we went straight for the faith and treat the entire group as terrorists. We didn't learn from the time we rounded up all those "Japs" after Pearl Harbor, did we? Now we say Rag and Towelhead as easily as ignorant Southern Whites referred to Freedmen as Niggers. We have forgotten one of the core principles of being an American... We FIGHT FOR THE WEAK! We are all American be it White-, Black-, Indian-, Native-, Mexican, Single-, Married-, Straight-, Gay-, Christian-, Baptist-, Muslim-, Atheist-, Handicapped- or (insert title)- American. It is our job to stand up with one another and destroy our enemies. I will stand with my brothers and sisters in arms against ISIS and any other faction but I will not hate someone for their faith. Just like I won't hate or condemn Christians for the idiotic, hateful actions of Westboro Baptist Church or any of the gay bashing homophobes who hide behind the Bible and the Word of God for hate. The attack on 9/11 made us forget that a person can be Black, White, Brown or even tattooed colored as a visual description, but AMERICAN is everything, every color, every background, every orientation. The saying is, "United We Stand, Divided We Fall." There is a whole lot of falling going on and that is a shame. This 9/11 I'm asking you, yes Y-O-U, "Are you representing a nation or are you representing simply yourself?" It's time to stop attacking ourselves and to start picking up the pieces for this nation and its people. Just a thought, friends!

Sept 11, 2015

*****

Once again, another preventable tragedy has struck our nation. A gunman opened fire on innocent people killing several, physically wounding more and mentally wounding even more than that. The fact it happens so often is an indication that we are in a bad place as a nation. The fact that the bodies, once again, aren't even cold yet and Facebook blew up with idiotic memes defending "my rights as a gun owner" and "(insert rant) F Obama" is an indication that Americans have no idea what freedom nor the Constitution really means.

First, the problem isn't the men and women who love guns and have a fricken arsenal in their homes. Equally so the problem isn't those who despise weapons and only want peace and harmony. Those are the two extremes for this issue. Neither one of those can see or understand the other side of the coin. As usual it becomes the "my rights" issue. The problem is the people in the middle who have guns out of fear, who have guns out of need to commit crimes, who have guns because others have guns and who have guns yet don't have the mental capacity to take care of bottle of bubbles let alone a weapon that could kill. Gun control is a thing that needs to be talked about and needs to be worked out. Control does not mean confiscation of someone's 50-cal handgun. If gun rights enthusiast actually worked to help combat the abuse of guns, we would already have made amazing strides in protecting our citizens. That being said, taking someone's guns that they legally obtained is wrong. We need better gun LAWS.

In California if you are a part of a crime that results in the death of someone else, no matter if you personally caused the death, you are charged the same as everyone else. I didn't complain about the 3-Strike Law in California because (1) I don't have any strikes; (2) I don't plan on having any strikes; and (3) I can give two-shits about someone who is intent on breaking the law and being in and out of jail. I am all for open carry and the right to bear arms. I am also for that RIGHT to come with responsibility and ramifications if it is abused by A-M-E-R-I-C-A-N-S.

My rights are very important, but I cannot call myself an American, a Christian (or other denomination) if I am not first concerned with balance of my community and the rights of others. Isn't it time to start thinking about how we can make life better for others? It is truly sad that freedom has become "I get to do what I want" to so many people. By the way, the Constitution that those forefathers wrote has been amended 27 times including the ones that made women and minorities equal citizens. Maybe we should stop picking out the parts of history that fit our personal agenda and look at the big picture. My thoughts are with those who have lost someone in Oregon and my praise to those who tried to stop another senseless act of violence. Just a thought, friends!

Oct 05, 2015

*****

A victim will always find a way to blame others for what is wrong. A victim will give you countless reasons of why "this person is undeserving" and why "these people are pathetic, useless, wrong, hateful, etc., etc., etc." but will never give a solution. A victim will cry for what they don't have and even defend that stance when someone points out the things that they do have. A victim isn't at fault. A victim thinks his or her way of life is under attack and thus needs to attack others to protect their way. A victim will throw other people under the bus when cornered or in an unfavorable position rather than stand up and take responsibility. A victim looks at surroundings and says that he or she is powerless against the struggles be it poverty, drugs, hate, sexuality, religious belief and teachings, upbringing, social and economic standings, and so on and so on. The world is full of victims.

Here is my declaration: I will never be a victim! No matter how poor I grew up or how much adversity I had to deal with, I am not powerless. No matter how many hurdles I have to jump, mountains I have to climb, every step I take is mine and mine alone. It is my choice and thus I own what happens to me. I will not hold an ignorant opinion based off selectivity or minimal interaction with a group, race or culture as the definition of said group. Bad stuff happens to good people and I have the power to fight the bad and push the good. I am not a victim.

To all, believe in your God(s) and stand in the glory of that belief. Share the love that it is taught and reflect that in your actions, words and spirit. Stand up and be brave enough to teach respect, etiquette, humility, strength, determination, hard work and integrity to those around you and expect nothing less than that from them.

Parents, do not make your children spoiled little brats who have no idea how to be adults. All that does is make them "dependent" on you. The goal should always be to raise them to live and be "independent" of you. Most of all, talk about what you love and believe in rather than what you hate and don't believe in. It is time to step back and kill the victim in us and start being the community that most of those religious teachings want, no demand, us to be. Happy Sunday, my friends. It's just a thought!
Nov 01, 2015

*****

First, my thoughts go to the people in France, Kenya and Lebanon who all suffered horrific attacks by the cowards of ISIS. Never shall we be too afraid to stand up and fight for what is right. I do not care if you are Christian, Catholic, Muslim, Atheist, Indifferent, White, Black, Brown, Multi-colored, Gay, Straight, Special Needs or anything else. I will defend your right to live and be part of a society that embraces differences while maintaining respect and understanding of each other. Every time something like this happens people start screaming about killing the bastards and going to get them. I would deploy today, right now, if called upon to combat this cowardly group. That being said, I am sick of seeing politicians and people who sit back and suck the tit of freedom yelling how we need to send troops into countries to kill these bastards. If you really want to do it then get up and be a part of it or as Colonel Jessep said, "Grab a weapon and stand a post!" Don't just be outraged from the comforts of your home sipping on your "why they hate Christmas" Starbucks double-caf latte or using it to show how (whatever politician or political party you hate) has helped cause this to happen. No, get up and do something more than changing your picture. Men and women of the Armed Forces are ready to go into battle but I will be damned if I see another brother or sister in arms killed because we once again simply reacted like an angry mob with no sense of intelligence.

When we went into Iraq after 9/11 my good friend David said he was unhappy with President Bush's plan because "there is no exit strategy nor a plan to attack Al Qaeda and Sadaam." He was right. We fought a war with no real end for success in sight. I have personally seen too many flag-draped coffins loaded on the back of C-17s and C-130s to last a lifetime. ISIS has made its mark and today we stand as a world needing to get rid of a parasite that threatens every culture and everyone's freedom.

Yes, let us go and take care of this once and for all but let us also remember that peace has never been attained with killing. We made this monster and now we must deal with it because that is our burden to carry. May we remember that going "to get 'em" means our men and women will put their lives on the line once again for our freedoms. Hopefully this time we do it with the superiority that our Armed Forces have instead of going in like the movie *Ants* "Kill 'em with superior numbers." ... War has been waged and now we will see if all those chirping are really ready to pay that price... I sure as hell hope so! Just a thought.

Nov 14, 2015

*****

"I don't hate them but we can't trust them. Look at how they act. Look at how they treat others. They don't have a care for human life or dignity. Their ways are backwards. I don't want my kids learning that what they teach is OK. They are ignorant and savage. They have no honor and no real code. They teach hate and destroy anything that is different to their way of thinking. They don't look like us, think like us or have compassion and humanity like us. I'm not saying we need to kill them. Just that they need to be with their own kind in their own place or land. We must take care of our own, not because we hate them, but because we love what is ours."

Now, as you read that you probably are thinking Muslim or ISIS is the "them" and "they" I am speaking about. In part you would be correct. This sentiment, and some much worse, has become the norm speaking about Muslims in this country. Did you notice I didn't use the word Muslim in the quote? Instead of Muslim let's insert Jew, African-American, Black, Negro, Slave, Caucasian, White, Cracker, Mexican, Wetback, Asian, Chink, Native-American, Redskin and so on, and so on.

You see, since the age of man people have said this same thing about other races and cultures. Those pesky Confederates couldn't trust the Coloreds because Blacks couldn't learn and be dignified like the White Christians of the South. How about in the Black and Mexican communities where them White folks don't do nothing but want to beat and kill minorities. It's so good that people celebrate the death of White police officers. Oh yes, they can't be trusted. After Pearl Harbor good ole America rounded up all those evil Japs and put them in nice places until we could figure out who was a trustworthy chink. Can't trust a Mexican 'cause you know they are all illegals, rapists, murderers and drug mules. What's the point? Hate by any other name is still hate. Every time I see someone go on a rant about refugees, Muslims or the so-called War on Christ, all I hear is the same old hate from the many destructive forces from our past. The sad part is we are doing all this hating in the name of (your chosen) God. ISIS is using the Muslim faith to divide people and we are happy to oblige them.

So here I am a non-follower of any specific faith wondering where the teachings of the various Gods are at because it damn sure isn't in the actions of the followers of the respective faiths. Has our fear gotten so bad that we now can justify our hate and our evil actions?

Humanity is standing up for one another not standing back and picking a part one another. ISIS won't make me hate a person who follows the Muslim faith no more than the morons at Westboro Baptist Church will make me hate the Christian faith. A White man who goes on a racist shooting spree does not represent all White people just like some idiot Black who attacks a police officer represents Black people. If we don't want to be lumped into a grouping then shouldn't we stop doing it ourselves?

When we start to pick up each other as brothers then we will no longer be able to be manipulated by the few that wish to cause hate and fighting. Hate has never, and I mean NEVER, grown anything. I applaud those who would fight the enemy (ISIS) and still stand with those who are different from them. It is a shame we forgot how to love especially so close to Thanksgiving (or Black Friday, for most of you). Disappointed in us as a society. Just a thought, friends. Time to be better than this.

Nov 22, 2015

*****

I stood there with a boatload of people staring into the waves as they rolled on by me. Even though there was noise all around me only silence was closing in on my mind. Within a few minutes it was like I was alone in this place. I could feel the wind rip through me and the smell of explosions filled my nose and the cries of pain echoed through my ears. The radio calls I heard only a few minutes before now replayed in my head as those waves, so very peaceful with their rainbow tint, continued to ride the wind on by me. The whispers of the dead mumbled in the back as my mind continued playing this vivid movie of hurt, heroism, shock and resilience.

As I blinked my senses returned and I was once again with the crowd from the boat that brought us to this place. Kids running and people talking while a sentry stood guard. I made my way around and saw the names of the 1,177 fallen. Even as I sit here writing this post the chill from that day crosses my body and spirit because on that day, the day I stood over them, I could feel them with their loss and sacrifices.

On December 7, 1941 at Pearl Harbor the Japanese attacked us sending the US and the world into a tailspin that some still haven't recovered from to this day. The survivors from that attack are slowly and more frequently joining their long ago lost brothers and sisters who perished that day. Their voices will no longer be here to share the story of what happened and they, like the many others, will fade into a story of a time long forgotten. I was not there in 1941. For that matter, my parents were not even born yet but nevertheless their story will live on in me.

I don't know what happened to me that day I stood in the memorial of the USS *Arizona* but I am forever grateful it did. I am grateful because I remember and, on this day, someone reading these words will remember too. We lose so much in war and pursuit of power that we forget the lives that didn't make it out of the battle. Fair winds and following seas to all that died in the attack at Pearl Harbor. May we NEVER FORGET! Just a thought, friends. Dec 07, 2015

*****

First, Happy New Year to all of you! As I sat reflecting on 2015 a thought or, better yet, a question came to me. What if I did not make it through 2015? As I pondered that I wondered how I would be remembered by those that know me and by those that really only know a small part of me if much at all. After some interesting personal dialogue, I led myself (sounds funny) to the lesson I am about to share with those who care to read my ramblings.

How would a stranger or someone looking from the "outside-in" describe me if all they had was my actions to go off of instead of, as we tend to do, having to endure a million explanations and justifications of said actions? As I read Facebook over the past year I recalled seeing so many, as I see them, great people whose actions failed to reflect their beliefs, words, understandings, teachings and character. I found myself saying of people, "Oh that is (insert name), he or she is a really good person but is overly passionate about (insert cause...i.e. religion, politics, social standings, etc., etc.). It would be impossible for me to quantify the number of times I saw someone who spoke of loving God and then hating their fellow man. Then there were the countless people on both sides of the political spectrum sharing (sadly) what they knew were lies or misrepresentations of the truth in order to just throw dirt or discredit someone they didn't like or support. What would happen if we (you) were judged simply on the footprint we (you) have left on the world?

In 2016, I hope to see people being more conscious of the fact that screaming about your beliefs or rights is not the same as showing people through actions what you believe in nor that you understand that your "rights" have responsibility that we are all responsible to ensure.

We can all be better people in 2016 in all facets from religion to economics, but it must start with fixing the person in the mirror. Here are 7 suggestions to make 2016 better:

7. Take Out the Trash! - Don't forget the pain and hurt from the past because it was a lesson we needed to learn. However, DO NOT bring that pain into new situations. For example, just because your last boy or girlfriend was abusive doesn't mean that the next one will be nor should be treated as if they are the last. Toss that garbage thinking out.

6. Expand! – Don't allow yourself to simply associate with those of like minds and backgrounds. The best teacher of understanding is to sit at someone else's table not to judge them but to understand them. You very well may learn something about yourself in the process. (Challenge: Meet someone you normally wouldn't talk to and learn about that person.)

5. Embrace Magic(k)! – Life is beyond short. Stop rushing from here and there trying to get bigger and better all the time. Before you know it, you will be too old, too sick or too dead to actually enjoy the amazing things like sunrises, sunsets, waves crashing, playing with family, chatting with friends without checking your phone every 2 minutes, and so-on, and so-on. (Challenge: Find one thing you always wanted to do or try and do it in 2016. i.e. learn a language, try a new food, visit a new place, spend a day somewhere, etc., etc., etc.).

4. Laugh! – Laugh with people. Once a week spend time with people that make your heart smile.

3. Abuse the Light! –Instead of hitting "share" on that horrific story that promotes idiots, share the stories of

the victims, share the stories of people coming together and helping, share YOUR story of doing great with and for others. Let us stop blaming the media for all the negative and start showing the positive ourselves.

2. Let the Heart Shine! – Love is the one thing we have an abundance of to give, yet we share it the least. Invest the most precious commodity into people: your time, your attention and your compassion. (Note: Don't be used though.)

1. To Thine Own Self Be True! – Love yourself. The biggest lie we tell is the one where someone else is #1 in our lives. Number one has always been taken by YOU. Learn to love yourself and the love you have for others will be exponentially better. (Challenge: Do something solely for yourself. It is OK to be selfish once in a while.)
Jan 02, 2016

*****

First, Happy Easter to the followers of Christ who are celebrating the Resurrection. Secondly, Happy Easter to all those who celebrate this day for chocolate bunnies, baskets and family time. Thirdly, Happy Sunday to those who have no interest in this day of celebration or holiday. We all have the right to enjoy (or not enjoy) the day as we each deem appropriate, which brings me to my thought.

As you walk through this day be mindful that your beliefs, opinions and way of life are yours and yours alone. In our communities we must compromise to accommodate each other to the extent we are not being disrespectful to each other. Society has gotten so far away from brotherhood, community and fellowship (for the followers) that all we do is try to force "our" way onto others. Spend time telling, no, showing people why you love what you love instead of why you hate or dislike what you don't because it is in love that we can spread our joy.

It is disappointing to hear people of faith use their respective teachings as a weapon against those who don't believe what they believe. It is just as disappointing to see people who don't believe using the religious teachings as weapons against those who believe. Tell the world about your beliefs, your journey, your love, your struggles, how you overcame those struggles in such a way that others want to hear about it, not in such a way that others simply shut you out. I have unfriended or unsubscribed to so many people I respect or once respected because of hate filled rants on this media platform. I know what they hate, how they hate but have no idea what they love. We are all different, we see things differently, and that is what makes humanity special and wonderful. Isn't it time we resurrected the helping hands, social and cultural curiosity instead of the walls of contempt, fear and hate?

I wish each and every one of you the ability to sit and embrace someone who is exactly opposite of you. You might be amazed at how much alike you really are in the long run. Bring humanity back to the humans. Just a thought, friends. The picture was taken in Port Orchard, Washington on Friday night (Good Friday).

Mar 27, 2016

*****

I don't know if there is a heaven or hell nor if my brothers have made it to the pearly gates. What I do know is as long as I have breath in my body they will not be forgotten. I drink this cold one for MSgt Auchman, SPC Poulin and all those men and women who gave their lives in service of our country. As I pour out this offering for wherever your souls rest, remember one thing...you will not be forgotten. Ever!

April 01, 2016

*****

22-Day Push-Up Challenge

On May 7, 2016, I started a challenge of 22 push-ups a day for 22 days to bring awareness to the epidemic of veteran suicides. During the challenge I videoed myself doing my 22 push-ups. Each time I shared the video I wrote a message with it. The next group of messages are the path from day one to day twenty-two. Not all the days will be shared, just the ones I wrote messages on with the video.

Day 1

If you know me well, you know I don't personally post too much stuff in a day (not talking about responding to posts). I don't really do the hashtag thing (These are my first ever.) because really people are dumb with it and I rarely jump on any of these "causes" that so many people share on social media. With that in mind I bring you this video done by my Bootcamp girls this morning after they just finished an hour long Bootcamp session. I was proud to see each one wanted to join me in doing 22 push-ups.

The reason? To bring awareness to the tragic trend of 22

military veterans who take their own lives each day. TWENTY-TWO VETERAN SUICIDES A DAY! A person killing themselves is tragic all in itself. A person who sacrificed and was willing to give his or her life in defense of this nation killing themselves is beyond tragic to me. No one is alone, and no one has to be alone. We (military) never fight alone and we are not on watch alone. This is something that needs to be in the light of day not in the dark unspoken. Let's show that we stand for our men and women in uniform and they are never alone.

May 07, 2016

Day 2

Here I am with a Mother's Day message and 22 push-ups. Every day 22 veterans commit suicide in this country. As veterans, we know that number is unacceptable. That is why today I am doing 22 push-ups to help raise awareness.

May 08, 2016

Day 3

One person can bring awareness with a simple action provided that person believes in the purpose of said action. -Me

I won't challenge you by tagging you to do this. I won't make a spectacle or anything of that nature. I'll simply show that I was compelled to help bring awareness in a way that fits my style: by doing push-ups. Speaking for those who believed they could no longer serve our nation through push-ups is a small price to pay for the tragedy of another veteran life lost by his or her own hand.

May 09, 2016

Day 4

To carry a burden that is yours is to be a person living, but to carry one that isn't yours is to be a person most giving. Let not the burden you take from another person's stack, be the thing that takes your life and never gives it back. -Me

I won't challenge you by tagging you to do this. I won't make a spectacle or anything of that nature. I'll simply show that I was compelled to help bring awareness in a way that fits my style: by doing push-ups. Speaking for those who believed they could no longer serve our nation through push-ups is a small price to pay for the tragedy of another veteran life lost by his or her own hand.

May 10, 2016

Day 5

The decision to quit doesn't come from being weak but instead comes from not knowing one's own strength to persevere through the darkest of storms. -Me.

As I continue this challenge it weighs heavier on me with the idea that every night when I finally get my push-ups done, someone somewhere has decided life was too hard. It hurts me to the core to know that someone once wore a uniform and risked his or her life only to do what so many enemies had failed to do... take it.

May 11, 2016

Day 6

Never shall I walk into the darkness alone because of those that I love who wait for me to come home. Never shall I quit when the odds seem too steep because of those whose safety and freedom I promised to keep. Never will I forget the oath I stood and swore to defend because with that oath I will forever and always be a veteran. – Me

Here you are hopefully reading what follows. You and I have a choice to stand up and helps others fight or sit back and watch them quit. Life is worth living. Life is precious, and Death will find us all at some point. Let's not do Death's work. Stand up. Stand tall. Get help if you need. You're not alone because so many of us have your Six. Let's raise awareness.

May 12, 2016

Day 7

(Did this one on the shell covered beachhead.)

The greatest lie ever given to us was that of tomorrow because no matter the promise or how hard we wish, it will never come. Today is here and it is worth every ounce of your joy, so live it completely. -Me

Today as I walked the coastline I thought about the battle buddies I lost during deployments. The ones I personally knew and the ones I saw carried off the trucks into the back of C-17's with flags draped over them to find their families and their final resting place. They will never see tomorrow, the sunset, hear the waves or see an eagle fly overhead. They paid the price for our freedoms. It is tragic to see and painful, but we, as military, understand the burden we signed to defend. We did not sign to lose brothers and sisters to suicide. We did not sign up to watch one of our own quit fighting for whatever reason he or she has to do it. This is for them because one is too many. Let's put an end to this. By the way, my hands were gnarly after doing push-ups on those shells. Ouch.

May 13, 2016

Day 8

The journey to the end will be paved with challenges that may seem too hard to overcome, but no challenge is worth taking your life, not a single solitary one. -Me

I'm not sure how much of an impact these videos make on others but I know how much it makes on me. Every day I do these I think about how much someone must hurt in order to call it quits. I think about what it takes to make the choice to not see tomorrow. These push-ups are reminding me that I can't quit. I won't quit and as long as I have the ability to speak I won't let someone else quit without helping them fight for themselves. We should all be looking out for each other, not just us military people. Each suicide is a tragedy that can be stopped. Let's stop it.

May 14, 2016

Day 9

Some days you just want the world to stop hurting you on the inside, but when it gets too hard remember we will be there because veterans are never on a solo ride! -Me. United We Stand!

We all have times when we feel lost, afraid, hurt, empty, overwhelmed and even in a state of hopelessness, but those times can only break us if we choose to not believe we can stand up and persevere through them. One suicide is too many. Let's show people there are always ways to carry on and fight for their own lives.

May 15, 2016

Day 10

Here I am 220 push-ups into this challenge and with each day I am being brought back to the unity and community of my military family. It hurts to know that someone who I would go to battle with, risk my life for and vice versa would end it all by his or her own hand. That is a wound that cannot be fixed or repaired. We veterans should not be inflicting wounds on ourselves. Let's end this horrible trend.

May 16, 2016

Day 11

A gesture may mean very little to you but to someone else it could mean the world. -Me (and probably a million other people)

I cannot fathom what it takes to not want to stand anymore. I can, however, fathom what it takes to let those people know they are not alone. Let's end this tragedy.

May 17, 2016

Day 12

As I sit and knockout 22 more push-ups, I see that, by this number or average, that 264 veterans would have taken their lives over these past 12 days. 264! Can we really turn an eye to that number? Can we really think that 264 in 12 days is ok? Let's push to stop this craziness. We are all better than this, period.

May 18, 2016

Day 13

What does it take to let someone know they are not alone? In a world of instant connections, it is tragic to think that some people feel there is no hope, no way out, no bright light at the end of the tunnel. That has to change.

May 19, 2016

Day 14 and Day 15

Today I did 44 push-ups because no military person is ever alone. We have a buddy system and we check each other's six. Sometimes we need a reminder, so here is me tired and exhausted knocking out day 14 and 15.

For 22 years I served my country. For all those years I sucked it up when it came to being tired, deploying, long days and nights and countless missed family milestones and events. I wasn't alone in this. Each and every one of us did the same. We carried on regardless of what was ailing us. That is what we did without reservation. Some of us can't carry on, can't tough it out and don't know where to go for help or even know how to ask for it. I am doing 22 push-ups a day for 22 days to bring awareness to the 22 veterans who take their lives daily. Today, I did 44 because we are never alone. Let's stop this tragedy.

May 21, 2016

Day 16

On this sunny day in Washington I am left with the uneasy knowledge that someone somewhere woke up and decided today was going to be it. I imagine the pain that goes through the mind to see no other way but to end it and that saddens me. We are stronger than that. We are better than that. We deserve more than that... Plain and simple!

May 22, 2016

Day 17

The question, "What good does something like this do?" was raised to me. My answer is simple. Somewhere someone is sitting with thoughts of ending it all. Thoughts of leaving the world behind. Thoughts of forgetting all the people who sacrificed for him and her and with him or her. That person may need a sign that he or she can carry on. Maybe, just maybe, he or she will stumble across this video and decide to go get help instead of waving the white flag to death. That is why I am doing it. For the possibility that someone may change his or her mind. It's that simple.

May 23, 2016

Day 18

Here I am again. Alive and well. Was able to eat my big salad for dinner and now I'm having edamame and tea for a snack. I'm sitting having 4 Facebook chat conversations and one text conversation with friends all up and down the West Coast. In a minute I'll play Candy Crush and I'll make my playlist for my Zumba class tomorrow. I expect there to be a tomorrow. In fact, I take for granted that there will be one. However, today, this afternoon or tonight someone will decide there will not be a tomorrow for him or her. He or she will decide that enough is enough and end it all with his or her own hand and own choice. I'm doing 22 push-ups a day to bring awareness that there are people that you may know who are hurting so bad that the tomorrow I take for granted

they don't wish to see. We can help them, and we should help them... we WILL help them. They are not alone, and neither are you. Time to raise the bar for Buddy Check!
May 24, 2016

Day 19

To simply do a push-up 22 times doesn't take much. They help people to think of those who are hurting and in need of help; it is a gift that should be given. Life is a treasure and we need not snuff it out on our own accord but to live it until our time has come. One suicide is too many. Twenty-two veteran suicides is an epidemic in my book. Let's end this.
May 25, 2016

Day 20

If I were to ever be so lost that I wanted to simply make it all stop, I hope that someone would see my pain and help me get back on top. -Me.

Here we are day 20 of the 22 Push-up Challenge. I have said a lot in each of these posts, but the common statement is that no one should feel that overwhelmed that they would rather die than get help. No one! Let's bring this to light and let people know that they are not alone.

May 26, 2016

Day 21

Every day 22 veterans take their own lives. Twenty-two men and women who once served this nation could no longer take the demons within and could no longer fight. We are there for them, but they didn't know it. We need to change that because no veteran is alone. We can do better for them.

May 29, 2016

Day 22

(Only a video message)

Addition: On this day I did my last 22 push-ups in the Retsil Veterans Cemetery here in Port Orchard, Washington. If you noticed the days skipped which was on purpose because I wanted to end Day 22 on Memorial Day. The journey changed me. I cannot explain what it meant to take a moment to acknowledge the pain of others day after day. I carry on now because of those who couldn't or wouldn't carry on.

This additional message is written May 21, 2018.

Original message was May 30, 2016.

> And that concluded the 22-day challenge to bring awareness for veteran suicides.

*****

It has been a while since I've done one of these mainly because I'm still shaking my head at what society has devolved into. Another senseless tragedy has hit this planet. No, it isn't just an American thing; it's a world thing. And the first thing I see is Muslim hate, gun hate, gun rights, Obama hate and a myriad of political agenda posts. What happened to the world? Simple, we started caring solely about what is important for ourselves. The bodies of the dead aren't even cold, yet people are yelling about why they should be able to carry an AR-15. The wounded haven't left the hospital and people, no wait, a presidential frontrunner is tweeting about political propaganda. Let's be honest. No one gives a shit about those people in Florida. We only care about what is important to our lives. You can pray all you want. You can have moments of silence and fly flags at half-mast all you want, but in 2 days this tragedy will be forgotten by most with the exception being whichever group is trying to further a political agenda.

These mass shootings are a gun rights issue. They are not ONLY a gun rights issue. These shootings and attacks are a mental health issue. They are not ONLY a mental issue. They are religious persecution and freedom issue. They are not ONLY a religious persecution and freedom issue. Maybe if we stop looking at how this shit affects ourselves and start looking at how it affects our fellow man and woman then maybe we can make positive change for our world.

The sad part of all this is we the people have ourselves to blame. We want freedom of everything because any rule put in place is obviously an infringement on our rights. That's why someone can walk into a club and kill 50 people. That is why someone can walk into a school and kill a dozen or more children. That is why some radical religious group (Christian, Islamic or other) can use social media to recruit lost and misguided people to do what was once considered, unimaginable acts of violence against innocent people.

It is time to look in the mirror and ask the hard question: how am I helping to fuel this level of hate? If more people looked at themselves honestly, they would be horrified at the level of ugly that comes from their very being. This type of thing will stop when WE THE PEOPLE come together to end it, not one second before because, as they say, United We Stand and Divided We Fall! My thoughts are with the families in Florida.

Jun 12, 2016

*****

Fair warning. This is going to be raw (may have a bad word or two) and maybe long. I actually do not know as I am going to simply write what I need to say. So here we go...

I grew up in South Central Los Angeles and I HATED the police. White cops were racist and Black cops were sellouts trying to prove something to the White cops. This was my truth growing up. I didn't get that hate from my parents. My mother never spoke negatively about the police. My father, who had his share of run-ins with the police, never said anything bad enough to make me hate the police, but I did, like many of the other people in my neighborhood. All this came to mind as I watched another Black man shot and killed by police officers. It all came to mind when I saw police officers shot and killed by a Black man. The circle, the cycle, the hate, the victimization and rationalization of ignorance all came to mind. You see, I hated the police because that's what the "streets" taught us young Black and Hispanic people of LA. It was the criminals who yelled it loudest. It was the gang bangers and drug dealers always talking about police brutality. It was the former inmates who preached that we were being targeted and profiled. I believed it. I lived it. I saw every time a cop pulled someone over that the cop was wrong and the person was being picked on, profiled or just plain railroaded. That is the mentality of the hood. I grew up with it and I believed that the men and women in uniform weren't there to serve and protect but to execute and control. NWA's song "Fuck the Police" brought it home for me and I, along my friends, bought it. We bought it. Every single bullshit line that my life was being targeted for no reason whatsoever, I believed. And because of that I fought the police. I called them racist slurs, homophobic names, cursed their families and their Gods and whatever else I could do to show them I didn't give a damn. Luckily for me I never went to jail nor did I have a million run-ins with the law, but, then, I wasn't breaking the law. The best thing that happened to me was I left LA and went around the world in the military. I got to see how much hate was being pushed out towards those that risk their lives for the inner city which includes pastors, church groups, paramedics, doctors, nurses and even educators. I left, and it changed me to not see the Black and the White but more so the situation at hand. This is what I have come to realize.

No life matters. None. Not because police are being brutal but because citizens are being brutal. Oh yes, there are a bunch of shit bag police officers who are dirty, who are racist (not just White cops, by the way), who abuse his or her power but there are also much more who aren't those things. There are people who use race as a catchall for their own dirty deeds just like there are women who use rape or child alienation as weapons against mates that have done them wrong. We the people are the problem and it will not fix until we can admit what we each are bringing to the table.

Ever think that other people other than Blacks get shot and/or beat by police? Why are the only videos that go viral of White cop vs Black male (or female on occasion)? Because it keeps us divided as people. The same question can be asked about missing kids. Ever notice the only children that are missing that seem to go viral and be super newsworthy are little White ones? I cannot recall a time when there was a nationwide search or outcry for an Asian baby, Hispanic, Native American or any other kids except for the occasional Black child. Just like the fools I listened to growing up, all this selective media does is divide us, so we never come together as a people, better yet, as a species. Growing up, I never, and I mean never, saw that Whites stood by many of the Black civil rights leaders in fighting for our freedom. There are all sorts of races in those crowds, but the streets don't talk about it because hate breeds destruction and that's what it's all about.

I remember the coverage of Ferguson after the police officer was found to not have done wrong. All I saw was riots and property destruction by Black people. That was a small portion of what was happening. In fact, several days after, we started to see groups of Black men standing in front of the lines of police officers to protect them from angry mobs. We saw people come together to try and find an answer to humanity's problem. It took a long time, but we started seeing the truth that we all are better than that and it was inspiring because it is what we are, humans.

How do we fix the racism, the unfair and often unjust legal system, the imbalance of social and economic power in our country? The answer is simple. Stop being the victims. If a city is 80% of a race, then the police department shouldn't be 80% of another race. It makes it too easy to pull the race card on officers who risk their lives to protect people who, as a group but not individuals, hate them. If we start teaching our kids about what law enforcement, lawyers and judges and even politicians are needed for, then maybe we can get a better racial balance in those departments. We should be supporting locally-owned businesses. We should be teaching our kids how to work and earn respect rather than giving them everything including respect they didn't earn. If we don't, this road we are on will destroy us.

I don't hate cops anymore. I hate abuse of power. I hate non-transparency with traffic stops. I hate how easily both the officers and the suspect are manipulated for people's personal agenda. I hate that we, the people, are so caught up in looking at color that we simply don't see right and wrong. Make all police officers have vest cams that are reviewed by an independent agency instead of being kept in house. Make all citizens responsible for their verbal and often physical attacks on the peace officers. Create programs that help develop inner city youth into law enforcement, firefighters and EMTs by promoting the education for these services. All this hate is getting us nowhere and I am sick of it. Anyway, that's my rant, my friends.

July 10, 2016

*****

One of the problems with our society is how we communicate after a tragedy happens. When that occurs, there are really only two options most people feel they have: (A) defend their Point of View (POV); or (B) Express their POV. But what we need is a (C) listen to understand each other's POV, which brings me to today's point about Black Lives Matter (BLM).

I know some of you probably cringed just reading that line, others probably hit exit and aren't seeing this and even others may be open to what I am about to say. My last rant caused a couple really good conversations with a few friends from various ethnic and social backgrounds which is what open and honest communication should accomplish. The common theme I found was a lot of confusion about BLM and most of that comes from the media's depiction of this cause. So here is one person's (me) clarification for those who want to understand a little more:

As I stated in my rant from the other day I do not hate police, nor do I think they are out to get me. However, here is a truth that we, as a nation, cannot escape. The reaction of fatal violence is higher when it comes to Black males (specifically) than any other ethnicity. Growing up in LA we did see excessive force used on a regular basis by our police officers. No, not everyone was that way but the visual of being slammed to the ground, no matter the age or physical afflictions, was very real. As a young boy about 11 years old I stared down the barrel of a police gun because someone stole a scooter and we were all looking at it. LA specifically had an out-of-control Gang Unit in the Rampart Division that broke more laws than the criminals. That is part of the history that BLM is trying to convey. That is not acceptable to have trained officers resorting to lethal force as, for what it seems, a first response to escalating hostilities. That is, what being a trained peace officer is supposed to be about understanding when and how to use force. I personally know it is easier said than done, and often times we judge an officer's (or anyone's) action based on a clip or snippet but not the whole story.

It is the history that is the problem. It is the '60's with MLK and Malcolm that is the problem. It is the fact that inner city police departments are vastly different ethnically than the population they are policing. It is the perception of cover-ups and extreme sentences for crimes by minorities that don't seem to equate with wealthier and, to be frank, Caucasian criminals. Speaking of which, let me share what we see in the Black (and other minority) communities:

A drugged-out gun or knife wielding White male is threatening police officers. He is pointing his weapon at them, yelling, screaming, gesturing and the whole nine-yards. The guy doesn't get shot. Instead great care is taken to bring him in without harm or little harm. Shooting him is the last resort and it's often not 30+ shots that do it. Now, some of you reading may think that is hyperbole but it isn't. In fact, I have seen it played out on the news many times. Flip that script and make it a Black male and the outcome is expected to be much worse. That is the problem. We have come to expect it to be worse. That is what BLM is about. Equality of treatment. No one should be arguing against that, period.

Now, I can go on with a lot more examples, BUT this is already way too long for most people's attention span. So, I will say this, and I sincerely believe it, fighting for an equal handling of people by our Police officers DOES NOT give anyone the right to disrespect, target, attack and kill police officers. BLM is not about that. It is being depicted that way because it sells papers and gets clicks on websites. There are thousands upon thousands of Caucasians (and others) who have stood next to, marched with, protested with and fought with not only Blacks but other minorities, women, homosexual, transgender and any other group being mistreated in our nation. There have also been thousands upon thousands of Blacks who have stood up and fought for the men and women who protect our streets. The media doesn't show that, and we don't make it happen.

Yes, ALL LIVES MATTER! However, saying that negates the point of what BLM is trying to change, which means that we, yes all of us, are letting judgement and misunderstanding once again keep us from rising up as a people.

The last thing I will say is this, it is not only on the police departments to be accountable for their actions. It is also on the citizens to be accountable for their actions. As a Black man, I have seen way too many Black men killed by the hands of another and NO ONE steps up to do what is right. If we want to change the climate then we, ALL, must start changing it. It isn't us vs them it is WE THE PEOPLE.

Maybe this helps someone or maybe it doesn't. Either way I felt the need to share. Rant over!

July 19, 2016

*****

I am going to blast myself here 1 day after my birthday. Why? To prove a point, obviously. lol. Anyway, The Facebook memory thing is interesting as I just saw this post from August 7, 2013. Three years ago the post was valid and it is just a valid today but that isn't what caught my attention. How often do we say we are ready to do something? You know the statements like, "I'm about to get my degree", "I'm going to stop smoking", "I'm going to lose weight" or my personal arch nemesis "I'm going to write my book!" I was sure last year I said I would do that and while it hasn't happened I wasn't feeling anything bad about not succeeding yet. Then I saw this post and realized I said that in 2013. Three years have passed since I made the promise to myself to write my book. It is remarkable how fast time flies and how easy we can push a dream, a desire, a want, a goal to the side. I'm sitting here now shaking my head because I didn't even realize that it had been that long. Here's the question... What have you forgotten to get done?

It is never too late to live a dream. It will be too late if you never start. Reality check has arrived for me. Time to shoot that procrastination word and get busy. Thanks, Facebook, for memory.

Aug 07, 2016 (For the record, that book came out May of 2017.)

*****

When you realize the sunset is magical you do everything to capture it not realizing that if you did the magic would be gone. The wise simply enjoy it as it is, in its glory for as long as possible, knowing that they are better for the moment it was embraced.

Aug 11, 2016

*****

Dear American, please start paying attention to how ridiculous we have become and how easily swayed to a drastic opinion we are led. What am I talking about this time? The Colin Kaepernick not standing for the national anthem, and the "He is disrespecting the troops" outrage going on. Yes, I am purposefully a few days late because I wanted to think on it before blasting my Facebook page with a meme of the former 49er who gave up his NFL career and went into the military. There we go with comparing things that are not the same just for the sake of doing so. When will we learn? So here is my simple two cents:

I do not agree with the personal stand of Kaepernick. He is, in my opinion, wrong for saying he was sitting because of the "oppression" of the minorities in this country. First, no one is oppressed in that nature. Yes, racism exists and there are injustices that should be addressed and need to continue to spark discussion and action but not in a country where Oprah, Michael Jordan, Michael Jackson, Magic Johnson and Dr. Dre can all become billionaires (or in the general ballpark of one) it is real hard to argue oppression. That being said, Colin did not disrespect the flag or the men and women in uniform by not standing for the anthem. In fact, he did what we, all service members, have fought for which was his right to not stand. He sat quietly while the anthem was sung. The second game, during Military Appreciation, he took a knee. Not once did he do anything crazy or disrespectful during the national anthem. I may not agree with his stance but people calling him out as someone disrespecting our country is wrong, plain and simply so which brings me to the real problem I have with all this hoopla.

I have a question for those up in arms of Kaepernick's display. Are you pissed at every sign of disrespect to our flag and the men and women who serve it? If you are still reading my rambling you may be one of the "true Americans" who says, "Hell yea." Here is a list, as I have seen, that is actually more disrespectful than what Kaepernick has done:

1. Men wearing hats or caps during the national anthem
2. Talking during the national anthem of this or any country

3. Eating during the national anthem
4. Running for cover before getting caught out during the national anthem (This is a military one. Yes, it happens A LOT.)
5. Not stopping your vehicle (on base) during the national anthem

---- and so on---

But wait what about our flag? Here's a few for that one too:

1. Flying a flag that is dirty, torn, weathered and in disarray
2. Standing on the flag (Like those idiots trying to make a point for BLM early on in that movement)
3. Burning of the flag outside of a proper disposal for a flag no longer in shape to be flown
4. Flying or placing a flag of any kind above the US flag on US soil to include bases and housing overseas (It is amazing the number of Seahawks/12th Man flags fly above the US Flag here in Washington State.)

5. Flying those flags on the back of trucks that are draped over all the crap in the back of the bed or dragging along the dirty tailgates
6. Flying a flag in adverse weather conditions
7. Flying a flag at night without lighting

---and so on----

In the end, if you want to be up in arms over this, please be up in arms over the constant disrespect to our flag and the men and women who have served it. Such as seeing veterans homeless, without medical care, hurting and fighting for basic things promised them. Be upset about that. Be upset that many men and women are coming home addicted to pain pills, alcohol and drugs because of the demons of war. Be upset that the average American will never visit a veterans home to say thank you or to help out.

No, instead let's get pissed at Kaepernick for not standing for something so few show proper respect to. That is us as American. We are outraged, but as usual for the wrong things. It is time to wake up.

Sep 04, 2016

*****

We will never forget! That is what we say, the memes we share have pictures of the buildings or firefighters covered in dust and dirt or scared people running from burning and falling buildings. Facebook was quiet yesterday because so many states are suffering from natural disasters, recovering from them or preparing for one. Rightfully so, there has been tragedy after tragedy after tragedy hitting this country recently. Even with that I was left thinking about September 11th and "never forgetting" what happened. I realized the memes and pictures are lying. We did forget. We forgot in the worst way possible. We AMERICANS forgot about September 11th.

What did we forget? Terrorists attacked our nation. They didn't attack a Christian church. They didn't attack a Jewish temple. They didn't attack a Gay Pride rally. They didn't attack a pro-life or pro-choice location. They didn't attack a police station or fire department or hospital or clinic. They didn't attack a Black rally or festival. They didn't attack the Day of the Dead celebration. They didn't attack an Indian casino nor sacred grounds and lands. They didn't attack a Buddhist temple or shrine. They didn't attack a Pagan retreat. They didn't attack a school for wealthy children nor did they attack one in an impoverished neighborhood. No, none of those were attacked.

They attacked the World Trade Center, the Pentagon and speculated guess on the third location that wound up in a field. They attacked Blacks, Whites, Hispanics, Asians, US citizens, foreign visitors, tax payers, tax dodgers, criminals and law-abiding citizens, heterosexuals, homosexuals, asexuals, pedophiles and rapists too, drugs takers, drug dealers, Christians, Muslims, Atheists, Pagans, Satanists, Scientologists, rich, middle class and poor. They attacked the fabric of America. They attacked us. The melting pot. The "bring your weak, your poor and your tired..." They attacked the idealism of what we stand for as a nation. They couldn't kill our drive, they couldn't kill our fight, they couldn't hurt us and hope we turn the other cheek because this nation was built on war. The one thing we do is fight and fight and fight. So they attacked the fabric of what we are as a nation. We forgot. They succeeded with their goal because we forgot.

The attacks should have unified a nation. We were all attacked. Every group in this country suffered losses in that attack. Americans should have stood up and stood in front of other Americans who were being wrongfully persecuted in this great land. We forgot. We separated and segregated ourselves in religious groups, in racial groups, in sexual preference groups, in financial groups and so on, and so on. We forgot. The word "Muslim" became the "nigger" of this time. It became OK to scold, mock and attack without warning simply because of one's belief. We forgot. It became OK to want to bomb any and everyone regardless of the facts that lay before us because they (that enemy) was different than the group we rallied behind. We forgot. We closed our doors, we closed our minds, we closed our hearts and we forgot.

We said we will always remember but what did we remember? Did we remember what it means to be an American? We stand for the weak in the home of the brave. We fight because we have to, not because we can.

We attack as a last resort not a first utterance. We stand for the rights of each of us to have the same rights as we all have because we are American.

The natural disasters recently have reminded me what it is to be American and the thing we forgot from 9/11. As people rushed to safety no one cared if the person or people helping them were White, Black, gay, straight, Christian, Muslim, Atheist or anything else. They needed humanity and saw it in those trying to help them. From a group of self-proclaimed rednecks called the Cajun Navy to a Muslim mosque opening its doors for people displaced, to groups and individuals volunteering to help, we stood tall as Americans again. Humanity, humility and love were on display because that is the thing that couldn't be taken from us unless we took it from ourselves. We forgot that.

As I sit here now about to wrap up I think of the fallen brothers and sisters of my military family that have died since 9/11. I think of their families and their way of life that has been altered so much. I think of the people who have lost their lives helping others across this nation over the past few months and over the past hundred years of our nation. We owe it to them to remember what it means to be free. It means to stand together, to be one and unified. May we never forget again!

Sep 12, 2017

*****

(For the record, it's long and many won't like it.) It is amazing how easily people subscribe to slave mentality. How we, as a country, open the closets and dust off the old US vs THEM wardrobes. Yesterday I watched my Facebook and other social media platform blow up at all these disrespectful, whiny, rich, spoiled, ignorant, stupid, overpaid ass-hats and sons of bitches who should be fired. I watched people use their military service as a reason and pictures of fallen men and women in service as flags of proof and honor. I watched people tell about how long they have been fans of the brand and how they (and their families) will never watch again. How dare the NFL not make these players stand up, look straight and salute the flag? A very interesting thought that is and it got me thinking what was really being said yesterday from almost an exclusive group of people with a few exceptions. (I just saw a video of a Black man going off about these Democratic idiot ass-hats who got Trumped. That guy will be popular on both sides, I'm sure.) Anyway, back to my thought. What were we really saying with all this chatter yesterday? I'm glad you asked.

Black athletes, you are paid to play a sport. We want you to simply play that sport. You get paid lots of money to run around, bang against each other, flex your muscles, jump around and entertain us. We don't want your opinion; we want your physical ability. Run, fool. Jump. Catch the ball. Don't worry as long as you are good (and quiet) we will support you. We will buy your jerseys and shout your name. Don't worry. You won't get paid for those anyway but, hey, it is an honor for you to perform for us, the paying public. OK, hold on for a second that sounds a lot like something I heard in history class many years ago. Let me think for a second.

The owners need to keep their players in line. Players need to be appreciative of what we have given them. They are lucky to have these jobs and we can find more who will do it with respect. Owners should fire them if they do not perform the way we expect. What would they (these Black players) be doing if it wasn't for what the owners gave them? I know what it is. It is the slavery mentality. Now, I know some of you just cringed, a lot. Unfortunately, you should have cringed at the choice of taking that mentality. Let's look at what was really going on yesterday without the rhetoric.

NFL players took a knee during the national anthem (an MLB player did as well), NFL players locked arms in solidarity and some stayed in the locker room during the anthem (which was common practice until 2009 when the government paid the NFL to shuffle out them players to stand and salute for military recruitment but, eh, that's small potatoes). Correct me if I am wrong but not one player put a middle finger up during the anthem. Not one player told the military members in the audience that they hated them or they hated this country. Not one player spewed hate towards law enforcement or the establishment outside of many having a problem with our Commander-in-Chief lashing out at all those BLACK ATHLETES. Those players both Black and White protested what is still, shockingly, a huge problem in this country which is, in this case, racial inequality within the judicial system. You don't have to agree with those players but you do have to agree with one thing: they staged a peaceful demonstration which is their RIGHT.

Yes, they have the RIGHT as AMERICAN CITIZENS, no matter how much they make, no matter what their jobs are, no matter if they are poor and homeless or filthy rich living in a sky palace above some state. They have the right and I FOUGHT for it.

Yes, as a veteran, since everyone wants to use that as the reason they hate all this, I fought for every American's constitutional rights. I stand for the anthem because I did fight for those rights. I did have brothers and sisters killed in wars that made other people rich while leaving many of those very brothers and sisters forever wounded both physically and mentally, depending on a system (the VA) that is so flawed. I have yet to file my VA claim 2 years after I retired. Where is the outrage, by the way? Oh yea, it isn't a bunch of rich Black spoiled idiots so who gives a damn about that VA system.

I served so that the Nazis could have their lawful rally (provided they got the permit to do so) without them fearing physical attack. Yes, people have the right to counter-protest. They don't have the right to attack them physically no matter how much they may hate the speech. I served so that some White Confederate-flag-waving kid could walk into a Black church, execute 9 people, and still get a fair trial as dictated by our laws. I served so that a police officer would have to answer for his or her actions when it comes to the death of another person under his or her care no matter the race of the officer or the citizen. I served for some guy to overuse his 2nd Amendment right and carry a damn AK-47 on his shoulder because the laws in the state he is in says it is within his right. Equality is our right. EVERYONE'S RIGHT.

It truly breaks my heart to see people not even try to understand the "why". Why are so many people of a demographic, a race, a sexual orientation so upset? What can we do as a nation to right a wrong? We live in a country where the son of a rich man can be convicted of rape and be given 6 months of probation. While someone without the means for expensive counsel would get 30 years for the same crime. We live in a country where it is OK to tell Blacks to "get out" and "go back to Africa", but it isn't OK for those same Blacks to protest the injustices laid against them. We live in a country where we will forcefully deport people, break up their families and destroy lives because they are Mexican but have no problem bringing in foreign athletes who defect from their countries simply because they can play ball. I could go on forever but that isn't needed.

The point is this, maybe you don't like that these men (not sons of bitches) are using their respective platforms to force us to do what we are doing now. Start the conversations, challenge the system and make us deal with this bullshit underlying racial divide. They use their platform for those who don't have the money or the ability to do so. If you dislike that, then I guess you will no longer be supporting J.J. Watt who used his platform to raise 40 million (I think) dollars for Houston hurricane relief. That would be stupid of us to not support just like it is stupid of us to think that Americans should shut up and color because the government (in this case, the President) has stepped in and told them to sit, shut up and dance. No, that is not America. That is not what I fought for, and that is not what I will stand quietly by and watch.

In the end, sports is business and a business will succeed or fail. But as long as there are people there will always be a need to watch men and women compete. Don't fool yourselves. As many of the players have learned to do isn't it time we stood in unity for equality than this nonsense of telling people they don't have the right to do something that they in fact have the right to do? Make America Great! Not again, because looking back, it wasn't great for everyone, which means it wasn't great. Sep 25, 2017

*****

(Note: The video mentioned in this post was of long grass blowing in the breeze with the blue sky and sun behind it.)

Yesterday (Oct 3, 2017) I sent this video to about 10 friends with the caption "Vacation Stay" on it. As my friends opened it and saw it I got back the "hell yea" from some, the "oh my it's peaceful from others" and various other ways of basically saying they'd love to join me at that calm place. It is amazing. The sound of the waves, the birds and the breeze too. You can almost feel the sun warming your skin thinking about it. A 13-second clip could do that.

Now that more people are seeing it some may have noticed at the bottom of the video all the way across is what appears to be a line. That line is the Kitsap Mall here in Washington. This swaying grass in the sun was from the parking lot in front of the Buffalo Wild Wings. Perspective is something isn't it.

A friend of mine shared with me something her father told her. He said, "Be aware of a person's intent of what and why he or she is doing something instead of simply deciding based on the outcome." Now, I have used that saying 100 times and have reworded it every time because I could never remember it exactly. However, it is the backbone of what I am about to say.

In this time of hurt, anger, frailty and WTF-is-going-on-ness, we must slow down and realize a couple of truths. First, everything we see in the immediate aftermath of any event is completely slanted to the person's personal agenda. Memes, gifs, pics, posts and shares are all going to be that way. Second, information is given out differently depending on the audience and, therefore, if you lean one way or the other (politically so, in this case) the way something is portrayed will be either shown to solidify your thoughts on your side or to ignite your opinion on the other. Third, and most important, we are easily manipulated to be angered, to react and overreact and to not listen to other points of view or, as it is, perspectives. Last point, which brings me back to the dad's advice, is that someone could be sharing information that on its own is true but the timing, the reason and purpose (same thing in some cases) are for something other than simply sharing the truth.

We must, if we are going to move forward as a nation, sit down with people with opposing views, desires, understandings and wants than our own to learn and understand each other. In the wake of Las Vegas, I can tell you all the "gun control" talk is not going to reach the "2nd Amendment" folks at this point and vice versa. We are too charged and it is definitely not the right time to attack each other on fundamental beliefs. Oh yea, we need to have these talks but right now we need to support each other and the victims. Your perspective should be based on the whole picture of what happened not on bits and pieces of grass waving in the wind because what looks like heaven to some is actually hell to others.

Oct 04, 2017

*****

That was the very last "Sean's Thoughts" that was written. In January 2018, I started writing blogs (that will be shared in part 2), and inspirational posts (part 3). Now that we have completed the first part. Let us find our way to part 2.

*****

Part 2

When Thoughts Become Blogs

As I continued to grow as a writer, author and a motivational speaker I transitioned from random messages to blogging. What was once "Sean's Thoughts" evolved into what is in this section of the book. Unlike the thoughts from Book One, *Just a Thought*, and earlier in this book, these blogs are more thought out, use pictures and are, in most cases, longer. Even so, there is an evolution or growth from one to the next that I hope will be enjoyable and thought provoking to you. Enough of the intro. Let's get on with the blogs.

Take a Minute

Happy Monday, Inspiration Nation! Over this past weekend I sat in a booth with several independent authors at the Tacoma Home and Garden Show. As I sat talking to other authors and people brave enough to come check out our booth over the four days and many, many, many conversations, I had a thought which of course I want to share with you all.

What if we put down our prejudices, our assumptions, our personal beliefs and feelings for one minute? What if we did not see skin color, age, gender, sexual orientation, Republican, Democrat, veteran, hippie, nerd, religious preference, etc., etc., etc. for just one minute? What if you just saw a person who you were just meeting for the first time and the two of you got to speak without all that other stuff for one single minute? Kind of like a child would do. What would we learn about each other? What would you learn about yourself? If we put down all that we assume and know for one minute and simply are genuinely inquisitive about one another's life, who they are, what they do and vice versa, we would see how much more in common we all are on this big ball we live.

To a child, everyone is his or her friend. They play and make games up because that's what imaginative minds do. Yes, they fight, they argue, and they get mad enough not to want to be friends any longer and then they forgive. Sometimes it takes an adult to mend the fences but often without intervention kids will make up with one another. How much more would you understand if you knew nothing for the first minute of meeting someone?

Over the weekend I had the pleasure of talking to young and old, veterans and non-veterans, husbands and wives, able and disabled, readers and non-readers and all other types of people. And as I told my story of my book (and other's books as well) many were amazed at my journey to that point. Some walked away with my book and some did not, but all walked away with a different opinion of the big guy standing there in front of a book with him scowling on the cover. In fact, one guy said, "This can't be you. The guy on the book looks older and maybe a little angry. You have been smiling this whole time." I winked and said, "The book is about inspiration. The guy on the front was simply 'thoughting.'"

Today, I remind you that life is so much better when we embrace the unknown. When we walk and talk with strangers outside of our bubble and comfort zone. When we forget for one minute (and hopefully more) all the things we know to learn about the things we don't know. Be a kid and embrace the differences. You just might find yourself in the eyes of someone who looks nothing like you, acts nothing like you, sees the world in a totally different way than you do, while being very similar to you. Life is funny that way. Be amazing friends!

Jan 31, 2018

*****

Shut Up Already!

All my life I have talked. I mean, I HAVE BEEN TALKING! If you know me or have spent time around me then you absolutely are aware that I have lots to say about everything, anything and nothing at all. I speak what speaks to me. Recently, someone was watching one of my dance fitness choreography videos and said to me, "You talk a lot!" Now, this friend didn't say it in a mean way but more so poking fun at me for talking when I should be dancing. I thought to myself, do I really talk too much? It is not the first time someone has said such a thing to me. In fact, one of the helpers at an event I was recently at kept expressing how much I talked when people came to our station. Again, tongue in cheek? I really wasn't sure one way or the other.

I then thought about 2015 when I first came to Washington where a good friend of mine had been taking a yoga class in one of the neighboring cities. This friend is an early riser and can be a bit bubbly early in the morning. At the studio she went to, the owner was a self-proclaimed non-early riser. In fact, one of my favorite statements by the owner was "I can't be ON this early!" To say the grumpiness was in full effect would be an understatement. My friend eventually left the studio in part because her bubbly grand energy was too much for the owner to handle. Was she (my friend) being too much? Is that the same in the way I have been talking? After some deep thought I came to a realization.

Be yourself! Yes, that is it. That is the revelation. Yes, I'll add much more because writing is talking and, like I said, I like to talk. In any case, all my life people kept pointing out my faults, my shortcomings and my ability to yap. I wasn't trying to be anything special or act more important than anyone else. I just like to talk to people. Hell, I talk to myself when I am alone at home which, if you ask me, are grand conversations. Like my friend who is bubbly and full of energy at six in the morning I am a talker and communicator the moment my eyes open. That is my truth.

It has taken years to understand that what is natural to my heart and spirit will be there no matter where I am, what I am doing or who I am with because it is natural me. The problem, however, is not that I am a talker. It is that people want to change that in some fashion to fit what they wish it to be. Within that lies a secondary problem we all face when dealing with others who feel we should, in my case, shut up or, in my friend's case, be less bubbly or turned off. Why does that person or person's opinion matter? Truth is, it rarely does but it does not stop others from sharing those opinions.

Someone will always want you to be a better you but in the way that they see you being better. Now, that isn't a negative thing per se, but it can be if it stifles the authenticity of who you are at your core. Wise people, mentors and leaders want to help you be a better you while supporting that thing or things that make you unique and are your natural assets and abilities. Very few people have succeeded trying to be someone else.

I have surrounded myself with people who help me harness my ability to talk to people, my ability to motivate and my ability to bridge social, economic, racial and other divides. They don't want me to shut up. No, they want me doing what I do best just like I helped my friend realize: be myself.

My friend now uses her bubbly personality to help people and in that people flock to her classes and offerings because of that very thing the other owner of the studio disliked. Her authenticity, drive, focus on others and energy have helped bridge many gaps from doing nothing or believing they couldn't do anything, to not only doing it but in many cases growing as a person from it. She is happy to not have let someone else stop her from being who she is because who she is now is so much grander than ever before.

As for myself, I don't talk for the person who has heard me 1000 times. I talk for the person who might stumble across what I said, wrote or recorded and could use the information. What the guy at the event didn't realize was that my talking brought in lots of business not just for myself but the rest of the crew too. In the end, being myself was the right thing, is the right thing and will always be the right thing to do. I talk. It is what I do and frankly I am really, really, really, really (my English teacher friend is hating all those right now) good at it because people talk to me. This is a reminder to me to be that one thing that I need to be more than anything: myself.

If you made it this far congrats because here is the pearl of wisdom I will try and pass on to you. Everyone will have an opinion of what you should and should not be doing with your goals. More often than not you will hear about all the things you shouldn't be doing. Take those things with a grain of salt. Listen to criticism, take in all suggestions and filter out what works for you and move forward. Be you. Do you. Do those things that you do naturally and work on those that do not come naturally. Never let anyone shut you up for being you. Know the difference between doing something for the sake of doing it (to keep up appearances and such) and doing something authentically for you. Be willing to understand when and where to be fully you, partially you or (self-chosen) muted you. There is nothing wrong with taking a few steps back to respect where you are or who you are working with but there is a lot wrong in not being true to you.

So, shut up already you naysayers because I got something to say. Just a Thought!

Feb 06, 2018

*****

Dig My Own Grave!

As I was perusing the world of Facebook I stumbled across a fellow author's post about a recent blog he had been interviewed in. In his interview he told part of his history which included, for several years, being a grave digger. As I read I came back to the image of digging a grave. I pictured me out in a field, sweat dripping from my brow, body sore, hands tender with shovel in hand, plunging it into the earth, creating my own rectangle bed for my afterlife slumber. Then, I pictured me sitting on the edge of that grave, no, my grave. The image was as vivid as if I were actually there out of breath and tired from the work. I wondered what I would be thinking sitting there on that edge of the grave? That question brought me to another question. What would any of us think or do at that point? That brought me to my blog and jotting down the thoughts as I simply sit here at my computer. Let's take a quick journey, shall we.

If you had to dig your own grave would it change your perspective on life? Humanity is full of displays of death and our own mortality but we, as much as we can, mentally avoid the prospects of dying especially when we are young in age. In this day and age a lot of young people don't have a will, life insurance set aside for expenses afterward, or an in-case-of-death plan for others to follow. We avoid it (death talk) until it hits us in the face with situations like the sudden loss of someone or someone close to us losing a battle with a disease or simply passes with old age.

In this case though, you can't avoid it. In this case, you have to dig the grave. You have to put the shovel in and here that familiar sound as the metal pierces the dirt and you scoop one load of dirt after another. This is your truth, it is my truth, it is our truth and, in this case, the grave will be dug. If you are like me, you can picture it. Does it scare you? Does it make you say, "Oh, hell no!" to the idea of being that close to the end game of life? Or does it, like the thought did for me, give you much more? Now, you may be thinking, "Damn, Sean. This is kind of doom(ish)." But bear with me for a moment because it's not that at all. In fact, I'd say it's the opposite.

Life is shorter than we ever imagine. We run through 24-hour cycles like there are endless amounts of them. Hell, even our sun, the life force of our system, has an expiration date albeit a few million years in the future. When it is all said and done and I sit with myself on the edge of that grave, I wonder if I would be happy with my life? See, that is the point. If your day came where you had to walk out and dig your grave what would you think about that question? That is a hard notion to process I am sure but if my "day" was yesterday I'd imagine I would have to answer, yes.

You see, life is about the moments we are able to capture and enjoy both by one's self and with others, the lessons we learn and teach each other and the times we fall so hard it is almost impossible to imagine ever getting up and then we do just that, get up. It isn't about how much money you make or how many things you have attained because none of that goes with you. It isn't about who feared you and who revered you. It is about who you sat with and grew with you as a person. It is about embracing all the wonders of the world and living in those precious moments of discovery. Have I done that? I like to think I have done a great deal of that, yet I know I could definitely use more chances because life is grand.

I'll depart with this thought, we will never know the day the last breath will call to us but we do know that it will come. Open your heart to the love of the world, open your mind to that which is not your norm so you may learn and laugh. Yes, laugh! Laugh 'til tears run out of your eyes, 'til you can't catch your breath because laughter is one of the purest joys in our existence. If you are lucky enough to not have a shovel in hand then you have time to be part of something magical, your life. Isn't it grand? Just a thought, my friends.

Feb 14, 2018

*****

Human Control!

I am sure you have seen the news, heard the reports, read countless memes, shared your own point of view, argued against someone else's point of view, maybe cried, possibly became fuming mad or just became confounded by it all with the latest senseless act of violence in America. Most of you reading this will already know, but just in case you hadn't seen it, I am talking about the recent high school shooting in Florida this past week. Oh NO, not another person ranting about this! No, my friends, this isn't a rant. This isn't an attack. This isn't me standing on top of some high pulpit trying to be preachy. This is, like I always say, "Just a Thought!" Take a journey with me if you will.

One kid came to school and killed 17 people on Valentine's Day. A day where we show a grotesque amount of visual love to those we, well, love. Most of those kids and teachers that day did not imagine they would be faced with their own mortality in such a fashion. I imagine most were worried if their boyfriends, girlfriends, husbands, wives or whatever were going to do for them on this day of love. One kid with a gun ended that. Unlike most cases, this kid didn't run nor did he hide after it. He was taken peacefully into custody. He is expected to plead guilty. Lives have been changed forever including his and his family's. Tragic. So many tragedies hit us as a nation and a world. So, there is your recap. Now, why am I blogging about this when everyone and his or her mother has been blasting social media with an opinion? Because I believe this is needed for someone if not simply for myself.

When the news broke the shooting, before the body count was totaled, before all the parents knew the answer of if their son or daughter was alive or dead, we began to react in the same we always do. You know, first it was the, "Oh no, my heart is broken. Thoughts and prayers out to those affected." Then that was quickly followed by the gun control vs. Second Amendment messages, which were quickly followed by who the shooter was, depending on the background of the shooter, terrorist (Middle Eastern looking), thug (Black looking) or mental health issue (White looking). Some of you may think that is an exaggeration but I implore you to go look for yourself. Then the last thing of the normal reaction is to start pointing angered fingers at some person, persons, group or entity that either caused it or should have stopped it. Same sheet of music every single time. A week from now, some people will still be talking about it, but the majority will go right back to their day-to-day lives. Rinse and repeat for the next tragedy. Humans doing what humans do and that is attack others. This is the problem as I see it: "Humans doing what humans do!"

Everyone has an opinion that usually ends with telling people on the other side what they need to do. If you don't like guns then everything is about gun control. If you love guns it is all about Second Amendment rights. If you are Republican it seems it's about freedom to own. If you are Democrat it seems like the government and the NRA are the problem. Then there are the people who blame big pharmaceutical drugs and other programs for all the mental health issues we are facing. These people will remind us how weak and fragile we are as people. What we never see is ACTUAL solutions to the problems. Just more and more ranting and attacking. My goal is to give anyone who is reading this something to ponder from all sides.

1. The 2nd Amendment is viable. Yes, we have the right to have guns. Taking someone's rights away is wrong, period. It is the same when people wanted to take away the rights of NFL players to protest for equality. (That comparison will ruffle a few feathers, I'm sure). Rights are rights. That being said, we forget that the word "amendment" means it was added, that a correction was needed, to the Constitution. That also

means it can be amended again. Hell, it took one of those to let America recognize that I am actually not 3/5th of a man but a fully made man. An amendment did that according to our doctrine. We need gun control. We don't need to take people's guns away but we need to make people accountable for their weapons and choices to own them. My solution is simple but not at all fully inclusive:

A. When a firearm is found that is unregistered, it is confiscated and destroyed, period.

B. Any gun owner found with ammunition that has been modified or altered to increase its lethal nature (i.e. hollow point or armor piercing) is fined and the ammo is destroyed, making it less easy to kill police officers doing their jobs.

C. Assault rifles must be registered and secured. If found in unsafe condition (i.e. kids can access it or take it to school), it is confiscated and DESTROYED, period.

D. All gun owners must take a weapons safety course and carry the certification like they would car insurance or CPR certs. Carry a gun without it, and the weapon is confiscated until proof of training is provided. Otherwise, after 30 days it is destroyed.

E. Background checks are mandatory on EVERYONE who has a weapon.

Now, these are ideas, but the onus of gun control needs to be put on the gun owners. If you care about your guns then care about the destructive force behind them. Responsibility starts with those who choose to carry. It is a right and with that right comes responsibility.

2. Parenting! It is my belief that the majority of these incidents happen because we no longer teach our kids coping skills. We, as a nation, have coddled and hidden the hard parts of life from our kids because, simply put, we are too lazy to teach them how to deal with them. The latest report I read said the Florida shooter had just had a major breakup which is suspected to be his tipping point. Now, I know that can change in a heartbeat, but it isn't uncommon with these acts. Kids are killing each other and themselves because they lack the tools to handle adversity. That starts with parenting. Parents are the

ones who need to sit with their kids and talk about how to handle being bullied. It will always be a thing. Talk about how to handle break up, failing, not getting what they want and being individually strong enough to do what is right even if they are standing alone. Several of the kids at that Florida school said they knew he was going to do something. KNEW IT! How much could be prevented if our kids were strong enough to stand up and do the right thing for each other? They learn that from their parents or guardian figures.

3. Stop being political. The difference between Democrat and Republican is who gets the money, the poor or the rich. Everything else is a variation of the same crap. Politicians work for their constituents AND those who fund their campaigns. To be shocked that there are very few gun reactions from them would be foolish at best. More importantly, there is no reason to react when most people who are outraged will fight each other and then move on. This has been the same reaction since Columbine. It hasn't changed so why would they go to war on something that people only care about for 14 days or

less? Politics have never been about right and wrong. It has been about sides and keeping a job. WE THE PEOPLE are what make political change. Stop the idiotic name calling and start trying to figure out what to do, as in bipartisanship, to help our nation, not just the part of the nation that matters to you.

4. Thoughts and Prayers! Wow, this is being attacked this time around. The reason is because they don't do anything. It is that simple. If you believe in a higher power then praying may be great for you, but action by the people is what is needed. Even if your higher power was going to change things, he or she would use the people to do it. You are the "people." We have been praying since Columbine. Maybe we should start acting and making changes ourselves. This isn't an attack on religion or religious preference; it is an attack on the notion that a higher power must save us from ourselves. No, that is our job. That is my job. That is your job. You want change... Change it your damn self.

OK, I can go on forever, but the truth is most won't read past half way if that far. We, as human beings, need to do better. We need to stand up for the weak and protect them. We need to get off our bigotry, hatred and judgmental bias and extend a hand to help one another. There are enough natural tragedies in the world like earthquakes, tornado, winter storms, cancers, accidents and such that we don't need to add to it because we are too weak to do what is right. This is on us, we the people, the fragile, the strong, the independent, the left-wing, the right-wing, the racist, the sexist, the purist, the sacrificers, the religious, the atheists, the men, the women, the something else's, the dark skinned, the pale, the intelligent, the illiterate and everything else. It is ours to fix. Stop being distracted by the noise and start learning what we can do. We need human control!

The last thing, I chose this image of this tree I took because it truly represents America. It has all these gnarly limbs reaching out in all directions trying to reach the light. Everyone doing his or her own thing. All of our personal beliefs have us as a limb. The thing is they are all attached to the same trunk. The trunk gives life to the limbs and vice-versa. Cut too many off the other side and the tree becomes too heavy, falls and dies. We must work together to fix these issues because both sides are valuable. Just a thought, my friends.

Feb 18, 2018

*****

The Inspired Road

This past weekend I got the great pleasure of working with other authors at the SoNorthwest Women's Show at the Tacoma Dome. We had a booth of 70 or so titles with several authors there to sign their copies and help sell books of those who couldn't attend. Most of the books are fiction, fantasy, mystery and the such. One author has a thing for dragons, even having a character whose body (or is it skin? Can't remember right now.) of little tiny dragons that come to life. Personally, that is both creepy and awesome. Another author has stories centered around dogs and wolf type creatures. There are steampunk authors as well. There are stories of murder and mystery based in the Northwest as well as stories centered around some of the national parks like Yellowstone. We even have children's stories of a wiener dog with wheelchair supported backend named Frank and his yellow bird companion named Mustard. It is our own little Northwest authors version of a bookstore. It is amazing to be a part of such imaginations. They create worlds for a reader to transport to and visit. They write to whisk the reader away. It makes me smile simply writing that because so many people LOVE to be taken away to far off lands of love, adventure, mystery and so on. That is the purpose of their stories and it is amazing. Then I wondered, what is my purpose of my book and message? That question brings me here today.

My book, *Just a Thought*, is not fantasy or fiction. It isn't a wild, vivid tale of lesbian pirates battling evil lords in space. (Side note: I had said to a potential buyer that we had every genre in our group and one of the authors said that she had never seen Lesbian Pirates in space in our group before hence the reference.) Nor is it a time travel adventure or any epic tale of race against the clock of life. No, it's simply a thought or two. The reader doesn't get the chapters or the character build up. It isn't a biography of my life telling of my hardships of a young black male growing up in South Central Los Angeles and the path I took to rise above the gangs, drugs and violence usually attributed to inner city living. It is just a book of thoughts on random topics with no real rhyme or reason for why then and why now that I wrote them. So, again, what is my purpose? My purpose, I realized, is simply to inspire!

As I posted on Instagram yesterday, "When one reads my book *Just A Thought* I don't want them to get lost in my world. Instead I want them to be inspired to explore their own world because of my thoughts. Let your journey begin!" That is it, I want the reader to be inspired to start his or her own journey. His or her own adventure. I don't want to take someone into my world per se but instead have him or her walk with me for a minute and talk, explore, share, grow and then go onto his or her next path of his or her own world.

You see, storytellers like the great authors I get to work with from NIWA spin tales of fantasy to make you dream, hope, love and such. They inspire others to imagine the possibilities of not only fiction but their own stories hidden within the reader. Heck, many of them started writing because of the stories they had read when they were younger that gave them ideas of their own. In those worlds that they were transported in they'd want more from the heroine or hero. They'd want to know why they do what they do or did what they did or, better yet, how they survived or will survive. Inspired to dream and imagine. It is amazing how one can get lost in these worlds.

I want to inspire people to live. To be the hero and heroine of their own real-life stories. To pick others up while building one's self from the inside out. To think. To really think of the impact one's abilities would have to make the world a more fascinating place. I, in short, want others to take my thoughts and start his or her or their own journey to inspire. We never know what our stories will do for others ,but if we never tell them, how would we ever find out? The world needs it.

Last point, yesterday (Feb 25, 2018) on the last day of the SoNorthwest Women's Event I was humbled. First, I met a young lady (14) and a young man (15) who came by our tables. These youngsters were vibrant and wanted something more. They had energy and potential just beaming out of them. Each one of them went and got their mothers from the booth they were working (The moms were vendors too.) so they could get "this book I have to have!" They wanted to read my book because they wanted to explore something more tangible than what we like to feed our kids today. Who knew I'd be "tangible?" They kept coming back to visit for the rest of the day simply to talk to us at the table. I did have to explain to the young man that he couldn't stay in front of the table forever since others needed to make contact with people too but that is part of learning how to be in a place and not interfere with others. In any case, I felt great because they made the choice that they wanted something more to think about. The young girl was, at that time, the youngest person to buy my book that I knew of and it just made me feel good seeing the young generation want to explore other ways of thinking.

I did say "at the time" because a short while later this very energetic Energizer Bunny of a girl came and spoke to me. She was 11 or 12 (I believe) and spoke with views on friends, school and the world like she had been around for 50 years. She talked fast and moved faster. She had a nearly uncontrolled energy pouring out of her. She bounced from one topic to the other as we stood there. She was taking pictures of all the books she wanted to check out at our table. She had been banned by her mother from buying more books until she made more money to afford said books according to her. She was funny. When her mother and grandmother came over to our table I felt inclined to tell them that she was a wonderful little spirit. She was, no, is like me. She was me at her age, full of life, energy, ideas, thoughts with no idea of how to control all that energy. I told her, "You'll get it and when you do life will be simply easy and amazing for you" because it will be. I have no doubt about that talking to this little ball of fire. Her mom decided to buy my book and another for her (to her surprise) and she, like the other kids, promised to reach out to me and tell me what they think.

I never thought there would be a day where I would say I "enjoy" kids but these 3 youngsters remind me that kids are reflections of what we show them and teach them. They reminded me of hope. They reminded of life. They reminded me that my job isn't to tell them where to go but to teach and inspire them to want to go. In short, to make their path. Maybe one day, they'll show me the path of their world that will inspire me to my next one. It's a grand world we live in.

And for the record I sold 31 books in those two days. It was my best two-day period since I released my book. The women came to read! Humbled and grateful, I am!
Feb 26, 2018

*****

What Do We Miss?

Over this past weekend (March 2nd - 4th) I had the privilege of returning to Ft Lewis Army Installation which is now called Joint Base Lewis-McChord to sell copies of my book. For those that do not know from 2000 to 2005 I was stationed at Ft Lewis during my Air Force joint-service Army days. Until this month I hadn't been back on Ft Lewis since then (Sept 2005, to be exact). To say it was odd being back to a place that meant so much to me and my career was an understatement. It felt good to be home again.

In any case, here I was standing at the front of the post exchange smiling, nodding and greeting whoever had the time to look at the guy with the books who was standing in front of the sushi stand. I stood and watched people for 20 total hours. Due to the Girl Scouts setting up shop in front of me, my connections with people took a major hit but that rant is for another day. By the end of my weekend I had 20 people purchase my book. I am grateful for all that did and humbled every time someone chooses to read my words.

Now, you may think that this blog is about how wonderful my book is or how people should buy it. You'd be right and wrong. This is about much more.

The lady in this picture happened to be exiting the exchange with her cart. As she feverishly typed on her phone she hadn't noticed I was even standing next to her or the display of books with my face on it. In true Sean fashion I chimed in, "If you going to stop in front of my table, you can at least say hello!" Startled, she looked up and saw the big jolly guy I am standing in front of a stack of books. She laughed and decided to pull her cart on over and asked what my book was about.

Now, if you have ever heard me talk about my book or asked me about it you will no doubt have heard something of this nature.

Her: What's your book about?

Me: Everything!

Her: Everything?

Me: Yes.

Her: OK, well tell me about it.

Me: Here's what I do. Before I tell you about it I'll ask you to open it to any page and read one of the passages. Then I'll tell you what my book is about.

Her: Any passage?

(Most don't know the format of my book at this point.)

She then opens the book and reads one of the passages.

Now, you should also know that to date I have only had one person not have a reaction to doing this little trick of randomly reading a passage. In most cases, some people buy it based off what was read and some simply say that it was good message or thought and keep about his or her day. Most people, though, have a reaction and 75% or so will actually buy it after reading the random passage. Those are pretty good stats in my little mind for sure. Back to this young lady.

As she flipped to her page she started to read. Two lines in she quietly says to herself, "God bless you!" As she finishes reading she looks at me and says (This happens a lot mind you.), "This is exactly what I needed to hear today." The post was on being patient with people. She had been going through some stuff and her patience had been tested. She needed a reminder. For her, God gave her that reminder. She bought my book that day. She asked if she could share the story of why she bought it, the passage that nearly made her cry and if she could have a hug before she left. Of course, I said yes but requested she take a picture with me since she happened to be the first person to buy my book at Ft Lewis. After the quick selfie she said she was glad I had said something and that she had stopped in front of me to finish her text. It made me think, how much do we miss because we are too busy looking down, in a rush or know exactly what we (think) we need? This is the reason for today's blog.

In this world we are in a rush to get to this point or that point. We push through each other as if we were hanging plastic slabs over the entry to a cold beverage room in a store. We don't care about the slabs just that we get our cold beer. If the beer was warm, then we would care about those plastic slabs that weren't doing their job. That is life as we have made it. Instant pictures, instant messages, instant everything but very little connection. We look past each other. And, truth be told, who can blame us? In this world of instant gratification everyone is selling something, wanting something or expecting something. That is the nature of the beast. For me, I don't mind if people don't want to buy my book. Hell, they don't have to talk to me at all about it, but I do mind people walking by and not even saying hello as they do. Simple connection.

See we miss so much because (like the bottom picture I took and chose) we are on a road focused one way into a fog. We can't see the amazing around us because we never take a chance on things outside our zones of comfort. More importantly we need to know that what we know, believe and understand are subject to change as we learn more, evolve as a person and explore things outside of said comfort zone.

So, don't be in such a rush to dismiss that old person who simply wants to chat. You never know what life lesson he or she can give you or vice versa. Don't look past the waves on the coast while you are rushing to get to a show on tv because that little break could be the very stress relief you've been needing and didn't know it. Talk to strangers, share stories, embrace the differences in people and for the love of Pete (Anyone know him? I don't :D) LOOK UP!

The winds of time will tick by and in time the grains of sand will diminish for each of us. When that last pebble trickles down into the abyss let it not be filled with regret and unfulfilled adventure but instead let it radiate a life of exploring, loving, laughing and, yes, adventure, my friends!

March 07, 2018

*****

Let Me Change the World!

When I started this journey of speaking and sharing my thoughts I had no idea what I wanted to do with it all. As I gained more success and more people reached out to me I started to wonder what my impact was going to be on the world. I listen to the positive motivational speakers and I see the countless memes and articles telling me to "be the difference." Be the difference! As more people waxed poetic about what I have done over the past year I started thinking about another common motivational statement, "You can change the world." That is it! I am going to change the world. I mean, everything is about that "Positive Mindset", the "Speak it into Truth" and even the ones that tell us "Winners Never Quit!" I can change the world, damn it. I can make it happen. During my 6th grade graduation we sat and said,

If I can conceive it and I can believe it

then I can achieve it!

Oh man, even my 6th grade sayings are telling me so. This is definitely what I will do. I'm going to take the bull by the horns and make this world a better place. I'm motivated to do it. To put in the work. To make a change. To put my footprint on the planet and make us all better for it. I have conceived it. I believe it. Now, with that good work and determination, I can achieve it too. In fact, there is no time like the present. I'm ready to rock!

Here I am holding the sun. I am ready. The world is ready. All I have to do is have that "Can Do Spirit." I hope you are now motivated like I am to change the world. To make it a better place. For you and for me and the entire human race. Wait! That sounds like "We Are the World." Actually it is. And actually I don't believe all that rah rah I just waxed poetically about. Why? Because I learned something very valuable over this past year. I just have to share with whoever decides to read my blogs. I can't change the world and I don't want to either and neither should you. Now, I know you are here probably for some motivation, inspiration and, as my book is titled, *Just A Thought* or two. Don't worry this isn't a bad thing my realization, In fact, it is one of the best things I have learned recently.

Imagine a field of wildflowers as far as the eye can see. You wanted that field to be plush green grass instead. You don't have big equipment or anything that construction companies could use you just have you, your ingenuity and your drive. You want to change it all because you can see what a much better place it will be

when it is all plush green grass. Maybe you find a riding mower or a tiller and get to work. You are charging forward and making big changes to the world. You are doing it. But are you? Are you changing the world or, in this case, the field? You are changing a part of the field and you have a long way to go if you are going to make your dream happen. BUT! What if you didn't try to change the world or whole field as the goal? What if you did the smarter thing and changed one section at a time? If you grew up around farming you would know they use grids to work large farms. The same applies to helping the world. You see I can't change the whole world with one fell swoop of my magic brain. I can't even destroy the world with one push of my mighty nuclear button. It will take time for it to be fully affected. What I can do is change one section, or in my line of work, one person at a time.

I realized I needed to be something more than a person set to change the world. I needed to be a beacon for people. I needed to be a place where people could learn or share or grow or whatever they needed to become better people. I had a picture for that! I knew what I needed to be. I needed to be this:

I needed to be a lighthouse for others. I needed to simply be a truth. A place to think. A place to spark conversation. A place to share ideas. A place for safety in conversation. I didn't need to change the world. I need to change perspective. I needed to change attitude. I needed to change frailty, falsehoods, self-destructive thinking and behaviors and, most importantly, myself.

If I want to change that field of flowers, I need people to help. I need a community. I need a brother- and sisterhood to come and work with me. I need to help one person see what I am doing and want to be a part of it. I need to spread my joy to others and in turn they spread their joy to others. It grows and we change one at a time. We become a movement. We become a force. We become people who can change the field of flowers into a gorgeous field of grass. The same can be said about the world. The same can be said about me, you, us, we and them.

The short and skinny of it is I can mow down the field with big machines and till the dirt until I am blue in the face. Then I can bring in trucks of sod and have my fresh plush green grass laid out in rows until the entire field was plush green. The land would look just like I always dreamed. I've changed it. I used great human brain power and tools. I would be happy. I would be successful. I would have changed it.

However, in time, no matter what I have done, the wild flowers will return. Slowly they will pipe through. They will find a way to regrow, and if I don't keep on I,t they will start to spread across my green plush grass. I leave it longer and they will take over all of my green. It will take constant work to keep it only green grass. Leave it long enough and all my changes will be erased. I can't make a permanent change that way. Changing the world is the same way. We can force it and it will bend but give it long enough and it will, once again, return to what it was before it was forced to change.

Today, I only ask to change one person. One single  person for the better in that person's own eyes. That is the trick to doing great big things in this world, changing one person at a time.

When I focus on just being an inspiration to one person in need then I plant a seed for the person to cultivate and let grow within him- or herself. If I take my time with the weeds in the field taking one at a time, I can take its claim from the soil and therefore plant what I wish there. I cannot overpower the weed because it will only grow back stronger. I cannot overpower the world for it will return the force at which I attempt to take control with ten times the energy back towards me. I cannot stand against that power alone. I need allies and in them I have an ability to change the world or in this case the field of wildflowers.

I now know that it is in me to be the change people need to see, to feel and to understand where I am coming from and how I got there. They need the example that made me who I am. I need theirs to learn what made them who they are and together we can make changes. Let's change each other because the world is waiting on us to make it a better place.

More than thirty years after my sixth-grade graduation I will change the quote we used to fit me better today:

If I can conceive it, I can believe it then I can share it, cultivate it and WE can achieve it!

There it is in a nutshell, my simple revelation of life. One life. One story. One change. One person at a time.
March 19, 2018

*****

I Forgot About Tomorrow!

Every morning my eyes open somewhere around 6 a.m. no matter what time I went to bed or when my alarm may have been set. I usually reach over and pick up my phone to say good morning to some of my close day-to-day friends. I say hello in some various form to my friends Beckie, April, Kelly and Holly, the last two being out of my state. As my friends chime in at their own pace I get to moving. If I see the sky (sunrise) may be great, I'll toss on some clothes and walk down my neighborhood to snap pictures of the sunrise or I'll jump in the truck to, as I call it, "chase the sun" by the water in Manchester or down Banner Road. Around 6:30 I'll hear from the last lady I talk to each and every day my wife who tells me she has made it to work. The wife and I text each other until she has to run off to a meeting or two or I have to go teach. My other friends I hear from throughout the day. I'll talk to other people too. Some of those convos will be casual conversations and some deep. I'll dance in my fitness class, I'll yell in my Bootcamp class (if it's a day I do that) and I'll make a few people smile or laugh. This is my day in and day out. Oh, I should clear up and say I do eventually get all cleaned up properly before I start my day. Stank breath and body isn't really socially acceptable in my world. OK, back on topic. Why am I telling you about my daily happenings? Because this morning's message from the wife was different. She said (Without giving it all. Some is private you know.),

I makes it barely! Muah.

Gnarly car accident... with large police response... They had to make a path for me.

(a little later) It was a fatality hit and run ped (for pedestrian)

As I sat down at my dining room table to start typing away on the social media I looked out the window. I always look out the window. We have a bird feeder that is always active. Like any other day I looked, watched the birds, listened to the rain and typed away. Again, it is my normal routine to life. Today, I sat and thought about a body lying in the road no more than half a mile away from where I am sitting. A body! It isn't even really light out and someone's world has just ended. It isn't a body; it's a person. Someone will not see tomorrow.

While I'm typing this blog my wife texts me that she heard it was a lady helping someone who ran out of gas. At this point, the story changes as facts get released, we all know. But for now, this is what I have been told: she was being a good person and helping someone. Wow, do nice things, we say. It hits home to me since I did the same thing for a young kid around 11 p.m. one dark and rainy night. It was just above freezing and this kid broke down on a dark road and couldn't get anyone to help. A pedestrian saw him asleep in his car and checked on him. He waved me down as I was cruising the dark and busy road. I stopped to help. I was out, in dark clothes, because that is what I had on, on a rainy wet night. This lady could have been me. Again, Wow! Here I sit not far from someone whose tomorrow will not come. It made me think of a series of pictures and posts I did many moons ago.

This is me working at my desk, also known as my dining room table, during the winter of 2016. Every day I am in

this position at some point and time. Every morning I hunker down to either work or simply kill time in this chair, with this laptop, got a new water bottle and the piano behind me is pretty much covered in stuff now too. My wife growls and grumbles that I've turned her dining room table into my very own personal desk. Especially since I have an office upstairs. That is the funny thing about life though we take for granted these things. This is me today. This is me right now typing away at this blog. Every day at some point this is probably me.

It is also you. Not literally, of course. You have those things that you do all the time. The little things that the people around you know is you. It could be your shoes always in the same place or the way you burst into a room when you get home. Whatever it is, the people who know you right now can see it because it is your today. The lady who was killed today had that too. She had a spot, a way of doing things, people she spoke to and shared with or even if she was a loner someone somewhere was used to seeing her. But tomorrow will be different. Tomorrow will be completely different. No, tomorrow will be the same but she will not be with any of us.

See what happens when the person is gone? The next morning everything is the same. Everything is the way it was just like in this picture. Yes, I'm gone but there is my

laptop waiting for me to type away. There is my water bottle waiting for me to quench my thirst. There are my books waiting to be opened. And in this pic even those stupid balls waiting to hit me in the head. It is all there but one thing is missing. Me! My friends would wake up at 6 a.m. and wonder where the text was. My wife would wait for a reply that won't come through. Yet, life as it was will remain the same. There it is in a picture; everything but me.

The lady who helped someone today will not be in her picture. Tomorrow did not come for her. She made me remember the pictures I took. The thoughts that went through my head as I snapped the set of three. So far, I showed you two. First, life as normal. I am there tapping away at life in general. Then life as normal without me. The last one is the deepest. It is the one I thought of when I read my wife's text. It is the one where I forgot about tomorrow.

Life will move on without us! It has to. One day my laptop will be gone, my water bottle too. My books and my everyday will be someone else's space. After a while the very essence of my presence will no longer linger in this room. It may very well be redecorated at some point.

I will have been nothing more than a whisper in a room that once held me captive for hours upon hours doing what I love to do, sharing the world with people.

(Since this is a blog, you won't know if it is written straight or in breaks. In this case, the last paragraph I stopped about 2 hours ago so I could run errands. Now, I am back in my chair to finish this blog.)

When I sat down to finish, another friend chimed in on Messenger saying how horrible her day has been so far and it's "only Monday!" After a few barbs back about it actually being Thursday, my friend said she was, "Trying to fix my stinking thinking." Now, this isn't an attack on my friend because we have all had rough starts to our weeks but considering my thought process for today, I responded with,

"Well... I know you don't read my blogs but the one I am typing now is talking about the woman who stopped to help someone who ran out of gas at o'dark-thirty this morning and got hit and killed. I'm pretty sure she would love to have a shitty day where she is getting paid. Good or bad is totes up to you. Yes, I said totes. Be negative and you will always find it (and it will find you)."

The simple truth about life is that it isn't promised. We spend too much time hating the gift we have and not enough time enjoying it. This unknown lady who helped a stranger will not see tomorrow. We are not promised it. One day we will, in fact, forget about tomorrow. Shouldn't we make today the best? I would wager she had plans for the weekend and things she was excited to get done. Again, shouldn't we make today the best?

I'll leave with one last picture that came to mind as I write this blog. Stop! Stop hating yourself. Stop stressing over small crap that won't matter when it is all said and done. Stop worrying if you look a certain way or if people like you or don't like you. Stop looking down at the ground when life is in front of you. Stop being a victim to whatever you have told yourself is holding you back. Stop taking those who stand with you authentically for granted. Stop and see that the person in the mirror is the most important person you will ever know because he or she is the only person you will spend your ENTIRE life with, so STOP the self-hate. Life is short and we owe it to ourselves to enjoy it because one stop could be the last. My thoughts are with the family of the woman who will not see tomorrow. May she be at peace. May her family find peace.

And now I stop!

March 22, 2018

*****

And We Carry On

Today is April 1st, 2018. For many people around the world it is the day to celebrate the rising of Christ which is also known as Easter Sunday. To those who celebrate, Happy Easter to you and yours. For others, it is a day of jokes and pranks as it is also April Fool's Day. To those who prank, don't go too far. Then there are the people who today is just another day in a long line of days. To you all, good Sunday. Then there is me on this 1st day of April. Yes, I will have an Easter lunch and basket with my family because my wife celebrates every holiday there is that she is aware of celebrating. No, I am not a follower of a faith but I respect the beliefs of others as they celebrate Jesus Christ and their respective faiths. I will not prank anyone today because I have never found pranks worth the hassle and people go too far in most cases. In most ways today would be my only day off from work, which I use that term loosely since I teach dance fitness classes for a living, yet I am grateful for a do-nothing day. Today, for me, is not just Easter Sunday or

April Fool's Day but it is a day of a different type of remembrance. Today, is the day I got the call.

This picture was taken a few years back in the Retsil Veterans Cemetery on day 22 of my 22 pushup a day challenge to raise awareness for veteran suicides. In case you didn't know 22 veterans commit suicide every day. My last video was in a place where men and women who have served this country lay. I thought it was fitting to be with them as I spoke of the sadness of veteran suicide. We should never go out this way especially those who served. Especially for those who lost their lives on battlefields across this globe which brings me to what April 1st means to me.

On April 1st, 2011, at Bagram Airfield in Afghanistan around 0400 I got the final confirmation that Army Spc

Dennis Poulin had succumb to his injuries from a rollover accident. This kid, who I would not be able to pick out of line up if you paid me a million dollars to do so, would forever walk with me. I, with 4 others, carried him onto a medical bird so that he could be taken to Germany so his family could say goodbye. There was zero chance he would live without the life support that had kept him alive at that point. I was responsible for getting the information for my unit. I made calls all night to talk to the hospital once he arrived. I spent hours contacting another soldier's wife to tell her that his (the other soldier) head injury was not life threatening and he should return to Kunar within a few days. This was my

job and, to be frank, it wasn't the best part of it. On April 1st, I relayed the message to Lt Goble that Spc Poulin was pronounced deceased.

Today, for me and many others, is about the memory of the people who no longer have the ability to do what I can. The people who no longer can carry on the fight for whatever he or she believes in. It is about a young man who at 24 gave his life simply by being the gunner on top of a truck that rolled over. He wasn't in a fire fight. He wasn't running into the shit to get a comrade out of harm's way. He was a top the truck scanning the horizon for potential threats. It was the same thing done dozens of times as the convoy rolled back to base. He would not survive that final drive. He did not survive that final drive.

Today, I have to remember him, a kid who left a mother who never recovered from his death and two kids who will never truly know their father. I remember him and this day that he gave his life. I also am brought to remember the second person that walks with me for the rest of my life, MSgt Steven Auchman.

In November 2004, I sat in my supply office in the 5th Air Support compound on Ft Lewis Army Installation like I had done nearly every day for 4 years. On the morning of Nov 10th (I believe) we were rushed into our meeting room upstairs for an impromptu Commander's Call. The mood, which was usually joking and fairly immature in our unit, was quiet and thick (for lack of a better word). As the room was yelled to attention we shot up out of our seats and assumed the proper position. The CO came in, put us at-ease and told us to be seated. Once we were settled back down he told us that our unit had lost a member, MSgt Auchman, during a mortar attack on the base in Mosul, Iraq.

MSgt Auchman was a radio repair guy or part of the "support" package like myself, being supply. He was not supposed to die. He was not supposed to face any real danger. Support guys and gals are "in the rear with the gear" as we like to say. The Tactical Air Control Party (TACP) guys, on the other hand, were definitely in danger all the time. They were in firefights and hostile conditions that death hung around and watched in eager anticipation of new people to pick up. It was part

MSGT STEVEN AUCHMAN
KIA - OPERATION IRAQI FREEDOM
MOSUL, IRAQ
21 APR 67 – 9 NOV 04

of the job. While we didn't want one of the TACP's to be KIA we wouldn't be shocked if it happened. Sad? Yes. Shocked? No. That is the nature of the beast for them. Combat units have casualties. Spc Poulin is part of an infantry unit; the potential for death walks with those men daily. MSgt Auchman, on the other hand, wasn't supposed to be killed.

Of course, we all know that war brings potential death and anyone can face his or her time but the point is there is an air of "not us" when it comes to the jobs that are in the safer locations. That morning changed that notion all together. Our small unit hadn't lost a person in combat. Our small unit hadn't had to face the true stain of wars in foreign countries. The support folks would never have imagined it would be one of us that would do it. MSgt Auchman, with 24 years of service, was KIA in a bunker in Iraq. In that room I sat silently knowing that my life would never be the same.

I wasn't there in the combat zone with MSgt Auchman. His death hit me but hadn't changed me unlike the night I got the call that one of my soldiers had been sent to the Bagram Hospital in critical condition. I remember Lt

Goble's last words, "B, he won't make it. We stabilized him to get him to Germany." An hour later I was in the hospital looking at the unrecognizable kid in the ICU with 800 lbs. of equipment on and around him to keep him alive. I would be changed forever.

MSgt Auchman and Spc Poulin are not tattooed on my skin but linked to my spirit. On April 1st, Veteran's Day and Memorial Day, I wake with the reminder that I live, in part, because they cannot. One 24 years of military duty, the other 24 years old. They are forever connected to me. I will not forget them. I will not let that flame die. If it is in my ability, I will honor them the best way I know how, to live and find the amazingness in the world. Sometime this evening, after we have had our Easter lunch I will go to the store and grab another Corona and have a drink with these two men because I never want to forget.

As I sit here remembering the call on April 1st, 2011, and the somber meeting on November 10th, 2004, I know this is what I am supposed to do. Remember these men because they, inadvertently, made me who I am today. They do not know it. Hell, they will never be able to know it but they have changed me. Truth is, I have no idea what MSgt Auchman would be doing today or even if I would have ever spoken to him again after he retired from the military. I have no idea who Spc Poulin would be today or, again, if I would have ever spoken or even specifically thought of him again after or joint deployment for PRT Kunar in Afghanistan. What I do know is that I know what they can't do and it drives me to do what I can. I am an author, wellness workshop provider and motivational speaker because I realized I was wasting what I could do while they could not ever do anything again. Actually, that is not exactly true. They can inspire. They have inspired. Yes, that is what they have done. They have inspired me to grow as a person, as a man, as a student and a teacher because that is how I pay homage to them and all those who have gone before us both military and civilian.

As you celebrate today, be it for, the rising of Christ for Easter Sunday, the jokes and pranks for April Fool's Day or it is just another day, remember, life is a gift. You have the right to explore it, to dive into it and to enjoy it. If you take anything away from this message take this, the best way to honor those you have lost is to live your life to the fullest. Celebrate them by living, loving, laughing, sharing, exploring, learning, embracing, educating and dancing, too, (Yes, let's dance as well.) with everyone you meet. Life is too short, time is too short and existence is too short to not make it the best you can.

Today, after I have finished my Easter lunch with my family, I will drive down to the store and buy those 2 Coronas. I will take them to the water and sit with their memories. I will sip one and open one for not only Dennis and Steven but for all those who have gone before us. I will remember them because they can't be here. The most important thing I will do is try to be a better person who helps make things better for others.

Until I can no longer do it, this beer's for you! Just a Thought, my friends.

April 1, 2018

*****

No One Wants to be the Bus Driver!

Back in the fourth or fifth grade my teacher asked us to write down what we wanted to be when we grew up. Now, I know most of us have been asked that and, depending on our age, have had many answers to it. At 43-years-old I still remember the answer I gave the teacher that day. I happily responded, "I would like to be either a policeman or a hitman for the mob!" Just like you reading this now, my teacher gave me a look of bafflement and wondered how I came up with those two very different career choices. Even growing up in Los Angeles where there is always contention between law enforcement and minority groups, I found the police profession to be honorable. I wanted to "Serve and Protect" as the side of the police cars stated. I wanted to wear a uniform and know that people would feel safe when they saw me come into the room. I didn't want drugs and drug dealers hurting people or doing any of the stuff I saw on a regular basis walking the streets of South Central Los Angeles. Of course, the teacher found that to be a great reason to be a police officer.

As for the hitman for the mob choice, I figured I could be a badass killer taking out bad people. As you can probably guess at that age I really didn't understand what the mob was really about and that, to be frank, they weren't going to let my Black self into their Italian club. Even so, I proudly proclaimed those were my goals in life. My teacher did her best to guide me towards more honorable life choices to go along with being a police officer like a doctor, lawyer, teacher or scientist making discoveries for the world. What do you want to be? What a question that is for a little mind.

As you read that did you think back to your own time of answering that question? I bet it ranged from superhero to President of the World. Some might want to be athletes or millionaires or space and time travelers. Some want to be parents, farmers and even own zoos, restaurants, bookstores and coffee shops. The dreams are vast and amazing when you are that age. Sometimes they are illogical and far-fetched too. Some might want to be water or a bird. Maybe energy or part of the sun. I heard one kid recently say he was going to be a statue forever and never move from the spot. Now, that is imagination and a kid at play but it still makes me think of all the things we come up with to answer that question. However, no one wants to be the bus driver!

In this world there are thousands and thousands of buses which have bus drivers. Thousands of them. We see them on the freeways, on the streets, at the schools and the stadiums. Everywhere. Yet, no one says they want to be the bus driver when asked that question as a young child. As a person taking a trip I see a bus like the one pictured and I think, "Oh yea, this is going to be comfortable." But I know not at any point of my life growing up would I imagine actually being a bus driver. Did you? Did you ever think you would want to be a bus driver? No one wants to be the bus driver.

As we get older our desires and choices of what we want to be change for many reasons. Sometimes they stay the same or evolve to greater. For instance, I wanted to be a police officer but I decided to go into the military instead. Here is a  young me during basic training in the United States Air Force. I was going to be a Military Police Officer but wound up being an Inventory Control Specialist (supply guy). Even though I did not become a police officer I was protecting people. I was serving my country. I was the guy in uniform that people would see and feel safe around. I was what I wanted to be just not specifically.

Ironically, during my military career I did, in fact, drive buses which would make me a bus driver too. Hell, I even flew an F-15 Fighter jet during an Incentive Flight which I was awarded a chance to fly in that amazing plane. I guess I am a pilot too. In any case, and back on point, my dream to be something was being followed in the best way I could make happen. What I wanted to be when I grew up, while slightly altered, was being lived.

That is what we all hope for ourselves and our families. It is what we optimistically believe when we realize our little boy can throw a ball harder than the other kids or our little girl can outrun all the other kids in her school and loves track and field. It could be academic, physical, artistic or musical too. We see it and we know that a dream can become the reality. It's our hope. It's our desire. Hell, we even say it's our destiny. "Work hard enough and success will happen!" I've heard that many times. Yet, no one wants to be the bus driver.

What is your point? Why did I just read 4600 words that don't explain why no one wants to be a bus driver? You see, we all start out wanting to be something. We dream of it. We hope, pray, strive and drive to become it. Then life happens. Babies happen. Marriage happens. Money happens. Health happens. Ideas happen. It all changes as we grow older because old happens too.

The kid above in the Air Force blue wanted to be a police officer or a mob hitman eventually made his way to being the man to the left. That man was a Navy Petty Officer who retired after 22 years never having arrested anyone nor killed anyone who needed killing. Nothing like what I wanted to be when I grew up.

People from my city who see me don't recognize the man who now stands where a wild LA kid once stood. Some ask if I ever became this or that depending on what they remember of the person I was when we knew each other. I tell about my stories of world travel, stupid and amazing adventures, pains as well as heart filling moments. In the end, most people will say I have had a good life and that I am, if they are religious, blessed to have lived it.

As I type I think again, no one wants to be the bus driver. These people don't see the bus driver. They see the man that served his country, has gone to war, has helped motivate people. They see someone whose dreams changed but they can still relate to because I took one of those positive steps. I am grateful I can look people in the eye and they know who I am and they want to hear my story. The kid grew up and did something to be proud of and in that my footprint is made with the option to get bigger. Yet, I don't want to be the bus driver. Let me finally clarify.

The other day a friend of mine told a story of stopping to talk to a homeless man and his dog. After talking to them she went about her way running errands. She decided to buy the man some food and some dog food for the dog. She found the man and the dog a bit later and joined them as she gave them her offerings. The man was grateful as was the dog, I'm sure, and so was my friend. While sitting there someone drove by and yelled, "Get a job, you loser." No one wants to be a bus driver! Did the homeless set out to be homeless? Did he answer the question from his teacher way back in elementary school, "I want to be homeless with a dog starving and begging for food"? I am sure that is not what he wrote. I'd wager he wanted to be a doctor or a lawyer or maybe a boxer, but not homeless. Not a bus driver.

The kid in the Air Force uniform and the man in the Navy uniform served this country honorably. He has ribbons, awards, plaques and a myriad of accolades. He, better yet I, am proud of 22-years of service. Today,

the picture to the right is where more than a few men and women who once stood proudly in pictures like I have now live. Homeless with starving dogs hoping someone will help them. A man or woman who once risked life and limb for a flag of freedom now risks life and limb for leftover bread. At 43, I have a house, cars, family and some (not much) money. My financial needs are pretty much met but I, like the man my friend was talking to, could wind up living in this picture. I would not have written that as an answer to my teacher, yet that is where I could live.

We are a society that looks at people as if they wanted to be where they have landed. Oh yes, many have made choices that led them to where they are and that is a very important thing for each individual to wrestle with on his or her own. However, it is up to us to remember that they never set out to be there. We look at homeless people, drug addicts, prostitutes, hungry, poor and judge them for who they are today but forget that years before they

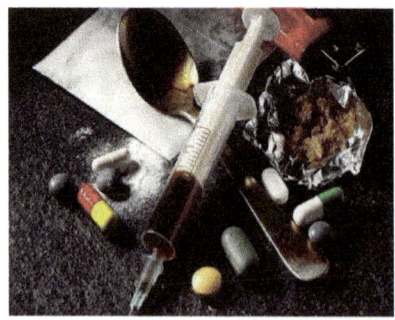

were kids in school talking about what they wanted to be when they grew up. No one sets out to be hooked on drugs. No one sets out to lose everything from money to hope. No one wants to risk death by sharing dirty needles and sexual acts with unhealthy and unclean people. They did not set out to be those people who become nobody as people walk by and walk over them. No one wants to be the bus driver. In fact, the beautiful hope that lives in us all for some burn like the bus here. It dies with the death of a parent, a personal attack, a lost love or, in a lot of cases, that first hit.

No one wants to be the bus driver when they have options to choose because we all want the best possible life we could ever imagine. Yet, someone has to be the bus driver. Someone is going to be the criminal, the  murderer, the rapist, the molester or any of the other evil things humans can become. They will also be the presidents, the doctors, healers, humanitarians, gardeners, bus drivers, janitors, athletes and everything else. Most will not be what they thought they would be when "they grew up" because life happens.

So, before you cast the stone of judgement at someone whose story you don't not know, take a moment and ask yourself, "What did he or she want to be when he or she grew up?" If we learn from other peoples' stories we may very well learn to help others who lost their way find it again. We all make choices; sometimes they are very bad ones that lead to a life of hurt, pain and personal destruction. My friend showed the example by simply being human to another person. Maybe we should try doing that more often to one another. Compassion takes little effort.

I'll end with this: I know a few bus drivers and they, for the most part, love what they do. We need them and we often take them for granted. They drive our kids to and from school, sporting events and academic events as well. It is an honorable job and my choice to use it was simply because no one has ever said, to me, they wanted to grow up and drive a bus. The truth is we should consider ourselves lucky if we could be the one to drive the bus.

It is never too late to grow up. What do you want to be when you grow up? For me, I want to drive the bus! Just a thought, my friends.

April 13, 2018

*****

One Full Circle in Place

It is amazing where the road of life takes us. We never know where we will end up or how it will turn out. What we know is that where we are today is part of a journey

started days, weeks, months and even years in the past. This morning I am sitting here a bit humbled and proud of where I am in life. Take a look at this photo.

This picture was sketched at South Kitsap High School here in Port Orchard. It is a sketch of me from the cover of my book, *Just A Thought.* The student who sketched it gave it to me as she left the classroom. It was a surprise when I saw and even more so when she gave it to me. Actually, it was super cool. Yes, Super Cool! Not for the reasons you might think either. It was super cool because of the journey that brought me to the point where this young girl had the opportunity to make this drawing of me. Let me explain.

Yesterday, April 30th, 2018, I walked into South Kitsap High School. I do this walk five times a week when I teach dance fitness and boot camp style classes for the staff but this day was very much different. On this day I walked into the main office to get a visitor's badge during school hours. This time, instead of a fitness instructor, I came as an author and motivational speaker who was going to talk to the class that happens to be reading my book this semester. After a few minutes in the office two eager boys each holding a copy of my book ushered me up to the classroom where I was greeted by my good friend April, a bunch of inquisitive faces, and a stack of books with my face on them. As I got ready to speak it dawned on me that life had changed drastically for me in the past 30 years since I was these very kids.

When I walked into the classroom a young man was sitting in the back row with his chair leaned back against the wall and his arms crossed. I recognized everything about this young man. The look, the swagger and the air of "I'm just here" attitude. He was me at that age. Now, to be fair to the kid I only made that connection from body language not from actually talking to him at that point. That being said, I am sure there is more accuracy in my thought than inaccuracies in that assessment. In any case, I told the kid to sit up and we got started. I surveyed the room as I introduced myself. One kid kept his arms crossed, hoodie on and looked forward most of the time as if I would turn him into stone if he looked at me. He eventually softened his stare by the end. Others were very interested in what I was saying and some might have been indifferent to it all. It was a mix and it was great to be there. It was also very strange for me.

See, 30 plus years ago I was the hard-headed kid who talked too much, cared too little and did almost nothing but disrupt my classes. I was a class clown, which in hindsight I'd change to simply clown, who wasn't worried about tomorrow or my future. At their age (juniors) I wasn't even sure I was going to graduate. Yet, here I stood talking to kids that were once me. In fact, my 11th grade year I almost flunked out because I skipped a lot of classes, did very little homework and could care less about any of it. I was lucky a gang problem forced me to finish my senior year at my dad's house in another city. I took 15 classes that year but I graduated on time and was kicked out into the world. Even now I shake my head yes when I think how lucky I was to have graduated.

Here I am in this classroom talking about life, choices, good and bad decisions and possible mistakes with kids who are reading my book. My book! I still can't believe that dumb kid from all those years ago is standing in a room helping these young kids with their perspectives and life choices. It is crazy for me to fathom. It is a shock. It is amazing. It is humbling. Me---a kid who heard his friend's mother tell her, "Don't play with him. He is nothing but trouble and will be dead or in jail by the time he is 18"---is now the man who is helping others avoid that very pitfall. The guy who is now in a framed portrait from a young quiet girl with blue (I believe) braces. As I told the kids, I would never in a million years think I would be an author, a motivational speaker, a dance fitness instructor and an inspiration to others. I barely made it out of school on time when I was their age and yet here I am.

Today's blog is a reminder to all of us that we have no idea where life will take us. We have no idea what our struggles will lead us to learn. We have no idea whose life we will change for the better or worse. One day we just may wake up having turned everything around for the benefit of others. In fact, you, yes, you, might be the one with a book that people need to read and a message that resonates deep within their beings making them better people. You never know.

This photo will stay on display in my house, not for vanity reasons, but because of what it now represents to me. It represents a life long journey to find the voice within me that speaks the truest and most authentic version of me. And by handing me that picture who knows what path my little lady with the braces will take next. Isn't life grand? I think so!

May 01, 2017

*****

Luckily, I Sit Alone!

I'm sitting here on this Monday morning sipping coffee (confession time: I realized I didn't have my coffee with me so I ran and made some so that line wouldn't be a lie. Integrity y'all! Lol). Yesterday I was in a restaurant doing my first solo paid-for workshop called Reframing and Verbiage. Four wonderful ladies signed up and spent 3 (actually 4) hours with me learning ways to identify mental, verbal and emotional pitfalls to our own health. We laughed, we shared and we talked as I gave them a few points that I personally find helpful. As they left I hugged each one, thanked them for taking time to join my workshop and then I reminded them, "Remember everything starts and ends with you!" What a phrase. Everything starts and ends with you? Even as I type that again I get goose bumps because it is one of the basic core truths of our lives. It is what I am thinking about this morning. It is what prompted today's blog. As I like to say, take a walk with me.

Last week I celebrated my friend's birthday by taking her to Alki Beach here in Washington State. My friend loves the water, good conversation, good food and great sunrise or sunset. Going to Alki Beach was a perfect way to celebrate her day. Of course, this isn't about her day but more so a picture I captured as we traveled along the beach watching the setting sun over the mountains. Before I do that I must say she had a great day. OK, back on point, as we drove down the road to the edge of the beach we stopped again (had stopped a few times to enjoy the sun set at various places already) where a bench near a bus stop caught my eye. I got out of the car and had to capture what I was seeing. Cars roared by me kneeling on the side of the road. People walked by, some watching the sky and others talking to each other or on their phones. Here I was in the street, in front of my friend's car, knelt down snapping a picture that was speaking to my very spirit. I snapped several pictures of it from various angles. I would send a copy of it to several friends reminding them to slow down, the world is an amazing place, or something similar. And I knew I would use it in a blog or a Facebook, Twitter, Instagram post at some point. Looks like the blog won out this time. You probably want to see the picture after all that rambling.

(A simple bench sitting at the end of Alki Beach overlooking the water at sunset. Photo by S. L. Brown)

When I saw this bench, I pictured myself as an old man sitting alone on it. Not sad or anything, just sitting taking time to watch the sky transform itself with every passing minute. I could see the years of life on my face. The stories both grand and harsh in the lines of my wrinkles. My grey hairs showing that life has indeed been lived for many years. I could see me. I could see the old man Sean just enjoying the view. That made me smile as I snapped pictures of it. The idea of being able to sit alone and enjoy life. That is the gift many of us refuse to give ourselves. The gift of being able to sit alone. I should say or point out at least that I did not say I pictured myself lonely or sad. I pictured myself alone on this bench. We must learn to find peace in the solitude of our lives. We must learn to embrace those moments when our spouses, friends, kids, co-workers and whoever else we have around us are not around and we are, in fact, alone. Can you picture yourself on this bench?

The truth is most of us would rather be surrounded by people all the time. We find joy with friends and interactions. We live and learn to love, if not covet, the noise and chaos. It is refreshing to laugh with friends. It is love-cup filling to spend adventures with those you love or even those you just met. Like I said, I had spent that day celebrating my friend's birthday when I took that picture. It was a great day of conversation, picture taking, great food and amazing sunset. My friend said it was a perfect birthday. I couldn't argue we had a great time that I was grateful to be a part of the celebration. There is nothing wrong with any of that I just mentioned. Adventures are definitely more exciting with kindred spirits. In fact, there was another picture I took during my trip to Alki that also spoke to me that represents this

sentiment   as   well.

(Four friends sitting on the wall laughing and watching the sunset. They had no idea I took this picture of them. Photo by S.L. Brown)

Many of us see life as this picture. We want to be surrounded by friends and loved ones and enjoy the simple life. I have no idea what these friends were celebrating or talking about but I know I stopped and smiled because they looked like they were having a great time. The picture would be amazing too if I could capture it which, luckily enough, I was able to do. They may have had the best day ever and that would be grand. I almost told them I took the picture and would send it to them but I chose to leave them to their merriment. That being said, this is what most of us want. I imagine a great deal of people reading right now could see themselves with a few friends (or family) enjoying this without much complaint. I could go on forever about simply living in this moment. I may have to take a trip and do it. However, this is about being alone. About the old me sitting and enjoying a bit of solitary solitude. Is that a redundant statement? Whichever it is, let's get back on track.

The person who learns to enjoy the company within as he or she takes the long walks on his or her own will then be able to enjoy the walk with others. Could you do it? Could you sit for an hour just being with the chatter of your own mind? In there lies the "what" I, over many years of contemplation, have found is the true inner peace most of us look for in others' companionship. The person in the mirror, the one in the same seat you are sitting, the one you do everything with 100 percent of the moments, days and years or your life from start to finish is the one you have to learn to sit with and enjoy. Find a bench to sit on and put the phone down, disconnect for a spell and just let your eyes, ears, minds, spirit and soul just be for a minute. It will be the best gift you can give yourself. It is the best gift I gave myself.

One of my favorite pictures to take are ones of docks or bridges. I can walk on dock on my own and just let the wind whisper to me, the water cleanse my thoughts and the sights give me inspiration of "what-ifs" that are out there. The bridge or dock often means someone is going somewhere. Where are the adventures they are going on? Where could I go? When I sit by myself I think of these things. The imagination walks in many directions and keeps my energy young. Look at these two pictures (below) and ask where would it take your mind? The first one is a favorite of mine because every time I walk it I become one with everything that is around me.

Where would this one take you? Would you find yourself watching the water wondering what all the sea creatures are doing? Or do you see the cars on the roads going up and down, back and forth, in and out and wonder where the people are off to? Maybe you'll find faces and images in the clouds or sit simply enjoying the solitude of it all.

For me, I do it all, depending on me. I think of conversations I have had or should have. I clear my mind of the chaos and enjoy the birds flying. I watch seagulls and eagles flying around, seals in the water and even boats, ships and ferries too. I allow myself to wonder where I would go if I was across the water at Bremerton Ferry Terminal catching a ferry out. There are no rules or limits to being able to sit alone, just letting go. The options are endless which is why this picture is a favorite because it looks endless.

Picture number two is a shorter dock and it has a surprise visitor of one of the Washington State Ferry. I sat at this short dock and pictured running down it and jumping on it. Guess I watched a few too many superhero  movies or something. Yet, here I stood at the end of the dock and the ferry just slipped on by. I pictured what would I do, where would I go and all the sorts. I enjoyed the wind and the sound of the waves. Even the shadows on the dock. Sitting alone allows me to let the mind go as if I was a child still full of wonder.

The question is, would you simply stop and enjoy a moment on your own? As I write I can imagine all the places one could go alone. Life is short. The world is hectic. People are chaotic. Danger lives around the bend. Love is grand. And, most importantly, adventure is everywhere. The life we learn to love the most should be the one that we hold deep inside. With that, I have one more picture to share.

When I sit alone and enjoy the world I often look at it like the picture I am going to share. I think many of us view life in this way. Some people would rather live it. Some would rather see the beauty of life in the distance rather than in reality. There is a difference between sitting alone and being happy with self and being distant and not being involved in life at all.

What do you see in this picture? Would it speak to you? Would it speak to the quietness within you? This is the culmination of the journey from my bench picture. How many ways can we simply sit and enjoy our "OWN" life and being a part of the amazingness that is the world? That is the million-dollar question.

I am lucky I have a great wife, great kids, great friends and, as an author and motivational speaker, a great little life. I don't want for support, or search or need for the connection of people. What I have learned, and hope I conveyed in this blog, is that for balance I also know I need more. I needed to learn to sit alone. Now, as you can tell from the pictures, I have learned to sit alone a lot because to be a better person for others I need to be better for and with me. This is my story today. This is my vision today. This is why I am happy today because "luckily, I sit alone!"

May 7, 2018

*****

One Year Today!

The morning of May 13 of 2017, a package arrived at a little house in Inglewood, California. The recipient of the package knew it was coming but did not know what was in it. The only instructions were, "Call me when you get it before you open it." This little package would be responsible for a world of change for many people. The sender of the package was me. The recipient was my mother Wanda. I waited and waited for the delivery to come. My mother wondered what in the hell did her son send her now. She was eager but not nearly as eager as me. Finally, she calls me and begins to open the package. She complains about holding the phone and trying to get through all the "damn tape" to get to it. She does not know what it is but she knows if her son, who doesn't call nearly enough for her, wants her on the phone, it must be special or important. I must confess, at that point I already had an expected response from her. She did not disappoint that expectation. As she opened the small package and pulled out the wrapped item and unwrapped it, she excitedly yelled, "Seeeeeeeeaaaaannnn, you did it!" To hear my mother filled with joy was my first goal in sending her that package. She was proud and I was proud that I had made her proud. On that day I think I won Mother's Day. Oh, you don't know what was in the package. What my mother was holding in her hand was my book. She had copy number one.

You see I wasn't always the best kid. I had my fair shares of dumb mistakes, lack of trying and failing to meet up to potential. I flunked classes I should have easily passed. I didn't get to college when I could have gone to any school I wanted if I had applied myself. My mother, like many parents, loved me through it all. My pig-headed boy days long passed. She had been proud of me and my life before she got that package mind you. I served honorably in the military for 22 years. I have an amazing wife and two pretty good kids who stand on their own. I've learned to follow my dreams and I love what I do. For her, as a parent, all she wants is for me to be strong, healthy, happy and doing what speaks to my soul. I think I'm doing pretty good at that so far.

However, this day she was standing happily staring at my face on a book, *Just A Thought* by S.L. Brown. Her son is an author. The woman who has a million books in boxes and on shelves all over the house now has one by her son, the kid who flunked English at one point. Took me 42 years to do it but I did something I'd never imagine doing. No one could take that moment from her nor take my published book out of existence. It happened. I am legit. What a gift. In fact, this picture of myself with the book and my cohort in crime April with the book is the actual first copy I got of my book that went to my mother.

I would have a picture of my mom with the book but getting her in front of a camera is like asking a dog to fly. Without serious help it just ain't gonna happen. We love her anyway. In any case, that was the Saturday before Mother's Day.

On May 14th, I shared with the world that I published my book. It shocked everyone that knew me that I finally did it. Of course, certain people got a copy (not many) and then others bought it that day or within that month. I have another confession, I was happy with making my mom and my wife happy that I wrote the book. Everyone else was just a great bonus. I had no idea what a difference a year would make. I owe a lot of credit to my good friend and crime partner April for what we have done so far from joining the Northwest Independent Writers Association (NIWA), being in Barnes and Nobles, signing events and even conducting wellness workshops to helping others build tools to be better for self. I would have never imagined being in any of these places. Even as I type and look at those couple pictures I am in disbelief that the two of us, April and I, have done so much in so little time. Here I sit, in belief, because I have lived it. I have met so many people and touched so many with my words. I, the kid who wasn't great to my teachers, have my book in the local high school class for reluctant readers. A few weeks ago I stood in that class talking about my book, my story and my life to those very kids. That my book and I are making an impact, still is a shock.

That is a huge shock, the kids loving my book, but there is nothing like seeing yourself on TV because of what you have done. A few weeks ago I was interviewed by the Kitsap Literary Artist and Writers (KLAW) group

hosted by author Peter Stockwell. I sat in the Bremerton Kitsap Access Television studio with April and talked about my book. In front of the camera with my writing as the focal point. It was surreal then and even now. The best part was when it aired on May 12th. Who is that guy on the big screen? Me! Just a

day short of my mother opening her book I am on television. Don't believe me? Check it out. I don't know if it is fitting or not but I find it remarkable the difference a year can make. And, after 5000 words I get to the actual point of today's blog.

Everything you read I am proud of and humbled by the fact that I, with my friend April, have accomplished with my book and my workshops. I never once imagined I'd be doing this or coming close to anything of this nature. That is the point. We all have dreams of doing something or being something but life, more often than not, may lead us into a different direction. Be free enough to follow what your heart and mind are telling you. Don't be so quick to hold onto one idea of what you "should be doing" so tightly that you miss the opportunities that you didn't know would take you on an adventure. Yes, I made my mother proud when she opened my book. Today, I am proud because I opened my mind to "possibilities" of life. When it is all said and done, I am so happy I jumped in!

I even have a picture to prove it. That guy doesn't like heights or really water he can't see the bottom of. Yet he did just what he feared and jumped in.

Where will you be in one year? Would you still be complaining about what you don't have, or will you be celebrating all the gifts you do? Maybe I'll be reading a blog about how you decided to take a chance and jump into the unknown and made a major change. I'd love to see that happen. Life is great. Live it!

I'll finish with this last thought. One day, no matter who we are, the road of life will end. For others it will carry on and in time the trail that was designed for me will be reconfigured for someone else to ride. Make the most of your time on the track and embrace building stories for yourself. When it's all said and done, those stories will be how you are carried with others in their stories of you. Live exceptionally simple, friends.

May 14, 2014

*****

What A Hug(e) Event

Last Saturday and Sunday my friend and biz partner April and I joined amazing author and inspirational speaker Simon Calcavecchia at the University of Washington's 40th Annual Street Fair. I was selling my book *Just A Thought* and Simon was selling his series *The Adventures of Frank and Mustard.* I think we need a little backstory before I carry on.

(Caption: April, Simon and I getting ready to change lives on Day 1 of UW Street Fair. Photo by S. L. Brown)

I met Simon back in December on 2017 at the Kitsap Mall where he and his illustrator Art (Yes, his name is Art.)

joined April and me as we sold books before Christmas. Simon is, for lack of a better term, straight up inspirational. As you can probably tell he is in a wheelchair but he did not start life that way. In fact, his first 19 years he not only walked but was a pretty good rugby player. At 19 (I reserve the right to be off by a year or two) he broke his neck playing rugby overseas. After some tough years he started to tell his story to people, schools and more. He realized that he didn't see a story of a kid in a wheelchair so he got to creating his series. His first book *Stuck in the Mud* is based on when he got stuck in the mud in his wheelchair. His second *Differently Awesome* is based on how he was included or not included because of his disability. He speaks at schools and motivates people by being simply a great guy, a joy with kids, motivated worker and, like I said, an inspiration. Check out *The Adventures of Frank and Mustard* to get more on this guy. It will be worth it.

In any case, when Simon invited us to join him at the street fair I said, let's do it. I had never done it before and he had only done it the year prior. This would be our first real event together. Full disclosure: I did not sell a ton of books at this fair. Just numbers wise it was ok in that I believe I broke even or just a bit better for overall expenses. Luckily for me though I do not look at it just like that because, although money is great, I like to change lives if I am able. This event would solidify that and then some for me and April. I can't speak for Simon but I am sure him too.

On day one we were set up next to a pretty aggressive vendor group. By aggressive I mean they were really pushing to get people into their area. Nothing really wrong with it except it caused many people to pass by

our booth without ever making eye contact with us. In short, it hurt our sales or, even more simply, our ability to talk to people. One of the reasons I like to work with

Simon is that he has a great following around these parts. He travels all over the West Coast talking at all levels of schools. People see the smiling guy in the pimped-out wheelchair and run up to him. It is odd not being the biggest person at the table but this dude earned his reputation and then some. In any case, I stand and speak to people. Simon does the same. April does the same. A great deal of folks just pass by looking like they aren't into anything at all. There are happy people and angry people all over. Simon is doing pretty well but, self admittedly, doing a bit slower than the year before. It is odd for both of us, if I'm honest, because we both have great personalities that people gravitate to but here we are struggling to get consistent connections. It is part of the business that we cannot fully account for that being people's interest in what we have to offer.

As the sun started beating on us we got more people to talk to us. Simon was, as usual, doing pretty well but I was still not having much success. The first thing that would change my day happened at this time. A young girl name Hamdi came to our table and asked about my book. I told her and she opened it. As I joked with her friend she went from one passage to the next. She talked to April, then her friend. She excitedly gripped my book and proclaimed, "I love this book. It is so inspirational.

With all I have been going through these past few years it is just what I needed to read." Now, I thought I definitely had a sale. April was smiling. I was feeling good then she said she couldn't get it at this time. We hear that a lot in our business, to be frank. Most people never get the books but some buy it at first chance they can. Hamdi lit up as she spoke about my book and what the 3 or 4 passages she read meant to her. She told her friend they needed to get it soon. (Now, I have to break into this story to say that when we unpacked I found a book that had its first two pages not sealed in the binding.) Simon says to her that if she really wanted it she could probably talk to the author about it. The light in her eyes and the smile on her face was enough. I reached over and grabbed the book. I said, "If I give you this you have to read it and tell me what you think. You also have to make her (the friend) get it too!" You would think she won the lottery with this one gesture. I am literally smiling writing that because it was so authentically genuine. She promised to do it all. In fact, she swore she was going to write long messages to us. After thanking me twenty times the two girls walked away. April stood there with her Mom-Smile being proud of me again. I was proud too.

This young girl made my day and time complete

ly worth it. I didn't make a sale but I changed a life. Yes, I want people buying my book. No, I will not give it away every time someone says they like it. I will, however, always stay true to myself. This young lady gave me a friendly reminder that sometimes you have to simply do the next best thing for someone else. She made my day.

I wound up giving 2 books away that day. The second was to a young homeless man who wanted to know if he could ride the bus to the public library in Port Orchard to read my book when it got there. From Seattle to Port Orchard just to read my book at a place he could afford?

Wow. I gave him my book and he put it with the other book he had in his pocket already.

(Caption: New spot, Day 2 and FREE HUGS! Photo by S. L. Brown)

Day one was a success because I helped people. Yes, I sold some books and had great conversations doing it. I wore people's glasses as we talked, posed for photos and joked with anyone who would talk to us. I told April that, "These people need a hug," which would bring us to day two.

Two very different things happened on day two. The first, Simon got us permission to move across the street from the spot we were on day 1. This provided us some distance from the more aggressive group. The second as you can partially see in the picture we offered Free Hugs to anyone who wanted them. When I say that one gesture changed an entire weekend I really mean it. Simon, April and I hugged well over a 100 people from little kids to the elderly. One girl hugged us both and simply said, "You have no idea how much I needed this today. Thank you!" Now you might think it was a gimmick to get people to buy our books. Actually it was, and it wasn't, because we hardly talked about our books to the people we hugged. If they asked then we talked about it. Some asked while others got their hugs and kept going. It wasn't just a gimmick it was, to be clear, amazing. Yes, amazing! We were changing people's attitudes with one gesture.

I hugged police officers, teenagers, couples, families and even groups of young men who had to "get some hug!" We started seeing smiles on people. They laughed and joked with us as they walked through. Many people told us that we were the best table there because we made people feel good. What? A simple hug or offer of a hug changed the moods of so many people. I think I hugged the guy in the picture (Martin) about 5 times because as I told people, "There are no limits on the hug amount." He cashed in a bunch with me, Simon and April. More importantly he and his companion sat and talked to us for over 30 minutes the first time down and 20 minutes when they came back.

We made people smile. Some did buy our books and some took our cards. I've even heard from a few since then. The funny thing is that we had amazing conversations with those who stopped for a hug. All it took was a sign to get people to change their mood. A simple sign, a smile from two jovial guys, a few jokes and a willingness to be open to something new. I stood up on my feet for over 24 hours that weekend but Sunday flew by because we engaged with so many people on the simplest level.

Now that you have gotten to this point I want to remind you that we miss out on so much when we get caught in our own heads. Life is about connection. We are connection. Learning each other's stories over coffee, food or even a good book is how we fill our cups with adventures. Take time to interact with people because you never know how they may change your life. A young girl, a homeless man and a bunch of people willing to embrace a stranger changed mine.

What a HUG(e) difference a day makes. Be amazing, friends.

May 26, 2018

*****

Lost on Memorial Day

(Caption: I stood under the flag and wondered what exactly my patriotism meant.)

Today is Memorial Day. Every year I write a post about my fallen brothers MSgt Auchman, Spc Poulin and all the other men and women who have died while serving or have served this country. I am normally pretty proud to stand up and proclaim my patriotism and my support to "never forget" these men and women who fought for my freedoms. I am proud to have served. I am proud to be able to remember the fallen. I am proud to stand and salute the flag and the national anthem because I served this country.

All that being said, something is different this year. This year, even in my pride, I am not happy. I am actually pretty sad looking at the memes, pictures and memories of fallen men and women all over social media. This last year has forced me to look at patriotism, sacrifice and what it means to defend the Constitution of this country. Even today, having only been out of bed for an hour, I have been bombarded with messages that make me question how we got so lost as a nation. I literally expect someone to blame President Obama or President Trump without thought. That is what it is about right now, finger pointing and blame giving. I could write fifty thousand words on all that but that is not what today's blog is about. Today, it is about Memorial Day and what I have realized over this last year more and more with each passing day.

The picture you see is from my very last combat deployment of my 22-year military career. At the time of the picture I had no idea if I was going to make it home alive, injured physically or mentally or something else. I was serving my country. My unit had already lost Spc Poulin in a rollover accident and even the SGM had been sent home from his wounds. Here I was traveling in country to be with my unit. What you can't tell is I'm thinking about my family, my friends, my battle buddies wondering if any of us understand what we are doing and why. I serve. I am proud to have served. I am proud to see those who serve and have served before me. I am honored to be their brother-in-arms. All that is in this picture.

Today, though, is Memorial Day and I am wondering about the flag that so many fly and wave around. I wonder about the sacrifices. This is the thing. Those sacrifices, that have me writing today because I think we forgot what the men and women actually fought for since the Europeans took over this land. Yes, we cannot ignore the truth of our birth as a nation. This land was taken by force and from it rose what we now proudly call America.

There it is from the beginning of our birth as a nation we missed the point. We are missing it even more so in today's society. Memorial Day for those who sacrificed their lives for our way of life is lost. We built a way of life, a core value (Constitution) and enforced it. Men and women died in support and defense of that very core value.

(Caption: Retsil Veterans Cemetery in Port Orchard, Washington. Photo by S. L. Brown.)

The Retsil Veterans Cemetery is on a road I drive often when heading down to take my sunset or sunrise and (hopefully) eagle pictures. One day I drove by and a mist was over it, so I stopped and sat for a bit. As I snapped a few pictures I wondered if the men and women buried there would be happy with where we are today. Would they believe their sacrifices were worth it? Would they be proud Americans or disappointed ones? I thought about it. I have not stopped thinking about it. I thought about Auchman and Poulin who never got to see life after the military because of wars overseas (Iraq and Afghanistan, specifically). Then I thought about me. What if LS1 Sean L. Brown had been Killed in Action (KIA) in one of those many places he wore his US military uniform defending his country? Would he be proud? Damn, even now that question makes me pause. I know the answer and it still makes me pause. The simple answer is, yes. Yes, I would be proud to have worn my uniforms and give my life for the ideals of this nation. I say that because of what I realized many years ago. That brings me to the point of this blog.

Back in the early 2000's I went home on leave where I got to talking to an old friend from the neighborhood. My friend viewed the military like most government jobs and agencies, as a place dominated by White people, for White people and, more specifically, rich White people. To be truthful that sentiment I've heard a time or two. He asked me, "Why the hell you serving this country that enslaved our people, funneled crack and drugs into our communities and treat us like second class citizens?" My first answer was that if we want to change the way the status quo is, we must be part of the change and do our part to be part of the solution. Now, on its own that is a great answer and really what we, as people all over, should be doing to make our world better. However, let me get back on track. That answer wasn't the epiphany. After my buddy and I got done talking I started thinking about it more and had a better answer for myself of why I serve(d) my country:

> *I, Sean L. Brown, serve my country for the murderers, the rapists, the molesters, the thieves, the abusers, the liars and the worst of the worst in our society. I serve so they would always have the right to fair, honest treatment within our systems. They would have a fair trial if arrested. They would have honest prosecution and a formidable defense. They would be innocent until proven guilty. They would have their rights afforded them by the Constitution.*

That is what I came up with in the early 2000's. Over this last few years, since my retirement in 2015, I have revised that to a simpler answer which is what I feel we have lost. I serve for EQUALITY. That is it. That is what the men and women have died for: the equal and fair treatment of EVERY citizen of this nation. That is what is lost. We lost the truth behind our laws. The truth behind our flag. The truth behind the anthem. Every one of them take second seat to the equality of our people.

I honor those who have died by remembering that they died for my right, as a Black man, to be considered a full man (not 3/5 of a man) in this country, a woman's right to decide what happens to her body, an immigrant's right to not be persecuted for taking the right steps to become part of this nation, a business person's right to honestly do business and earn as much as his or her hard work brings in and everyone's right to worship their god or gods of choice without persecution, demonization or fear of abuse from others. They fought for us to remember we, as a nation of multi-colors, backgrounds, ethnicities, orientations and abilities, should all have the same opportunities as the next person. And I THANK them from every part of my being because I do sit here as a man who stands with those who are oppressed, who are victimized, who are not equal in the eyes of those in power over them. That is what it is about for me. I honor them by standing up for those who don't have the freedoms that our symbols (flag and anthem) stand for in the first place.

I'll leave this with one last image. I flew 14 or so hours from the States back to Afghanistan with two pallets of coffins on board with us. I stared at the stacked metal boxes in the green light and knew that each one of

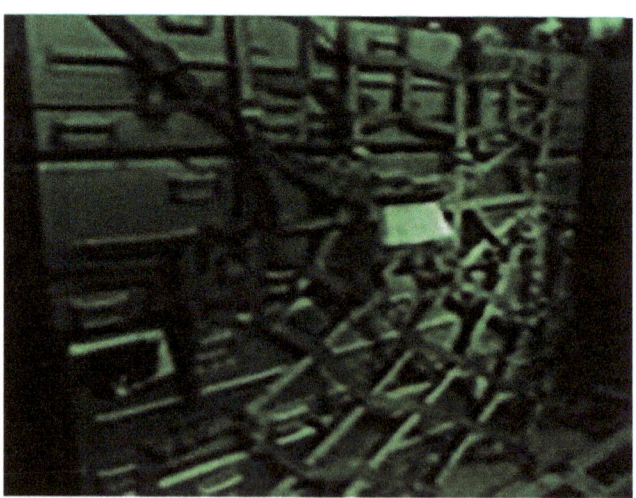

(Caption: Flying back from R&R with a stark reminder that death thrives at our destination. Photo by S. L. Brown.)

them would leave solo on a pallet going back. Inside would be a Soldier, Sailor, Marine or Airman who gave his or her life in the country. A person whose family would forever be different because of the loss. I flew knowing I still had 4 months to go and that I could very well be laying under the very flag that people are now using as a weapon against people fighting for their own equality. I couldn't have asked for a more in-your-face lesson of why I served than seeing those boxes on that plane taking me back to a war zone. I'll leave with this last line:

One metal box. One body. One flag. One nation. Equal for all!

To those who have died serving this country, I salute you. I hope that I am worthy enough to stand next to you in the afterlife having remembered what serving really means. Until then... Thank You!

May 28, 2018

*****

And in the Father We Find...

Today is Father's Day. For me it is any other day as I don't get to caught up in holidays of any kind really. My wife, on the other hand, loves all holidays and celebrations to the extent that she counterbalances my usual disdain for them. But, like my birthday, today is about me. Today is about men who have either had kids or are raising kids that are not biologically theirs. Today is Father's Day.

It is an interesting thing we do as society celebrating the fact that we created a little human. I mean it is our most basic instinct as a species. We must reproduce to continue our existence. We must have children to take care of us when we can no longer do so. It is no different than our need to breathe, eat or anything else. As a whole we must do it. That is at the most simplest thing that a father is, a person who made a child, raised a child, is raising a child or even mentors a child. In some sense all men are fathers at some point in their lifetimes. It is an interesting thing.

This year's Father's Day is a bit different for me because my youngest son Trae graduated high school this past Tuesday. For those that don't know, I have 2 boys. Trae is my step-son who I have raised since he was 4 (almost 5) years old. Sean, Jr. (who now goes by his mother's maiden name) lived with his mother and step-dad in England since he was 5 years old. My ex-wife is a great mom and her husband is a great guy. They raised my son to be a strong, caring, funny and loving young man. I have watched his life from a far. Seeing as he is all the wonderful things he is, I don't regret having to do so. Trae, on the other hand, has been with me and his mother most of his life. I got to raise him. He, too, is a smart, strong, caring and loving man that, like Sean, Jr., is off to college (Well, in August he will be). Trae has spent a lot of time with his father Mike and his half-brother, half-sister and stepmom during his life. Both these boys are doing what they want to do in life. I can say I am proud of both of them. I am also proud to know that Lee (Sean, Jr.'s stepdad) was part of his life. I am proud that Mikey (Trae's dad) was in his life. I am proud to have been in each of their lives to the best of my capacity. Most importantly, I am proud of the men they have started to become because that is what a father hopes to make of his sons... Great Men!

This blog will have (more than likely) one picture that epitomizes what I think Father's Day is really about and the purpose of today's blog. In this picture you see myself, Trae and Mike at Trae's 12th grade graduation.

(Caption: SKHS 2018 Graduation with Sean (l), Trae (c) and Mike (r). Step-dad, son and dad!)

His two fathers are getting to watch him take his next big step. It isn't about bravado or pride of self. It is about teaching him what it means to be a man. Both his dads are retired military men. Most of his grandfathers, some of his great-grandfathers, too. Yet, none forced military life onto him. Trae has traveled the world with his fathers, he has seen how we love, how we respect and how we stand as men. He has watched us deal with life's struggles and been by his side when he too dealt with them. He knows we are not perfect but demand the best of him. Better than we have been as men, as husbands, as fathers, as friends and as humans. We taught him to look people in the eyes. We taught him his word means everything. We taught him to stand up for what he believes in. We taught him to follow his dream, to love who he wants and to be whatever it is that makes him happy. We will support but not carry him as he transitions to the next chapter.

I look at the picture of us and realize that we made it. We made it to raising someone who is proud of himself. I don't know where Trae (or Sean, Jr. for that matter) will go from this point on. All I know is he (they) are equipped to do it. Which brings me back to this blog and the second point. To say Happy Father's Day.

So, Happy Father's Day to:

- All the men who made children and walked every single day with them in their paths

- The men who stepped in when no one else would or could and did what he felt was right

- The men who had to step out of the kids' lives and watch from a distance rather than have a kid raised in turmoil and hate because the parents don't get along

- The two-dad households because sexual orientation has shit to do with raising a loving kid

- The men who died before ever laying eyes on their kids or being able to see their kids grow up

- The men who failed miserably at being a dad no matter if it was drugs, drinking or some other vice that damaged their relationships yet the kid still grew up to be something

(Note: Sometimes the darkest of paths make the brightest of flowers. Hard family life doesn't mean a crappy adult life, daddy-issues or anything like that.

Damaged fathers also teach lessons. Sometimes it is simply "how not to be" in life.)

- The men taking time to coach teams, work at boys and girls clubs, mentor, church mentors or any other community type service
- The men who lead life by example in jobs of honor like military, doctors, police officers, (Yes, it is a great profession still.) writers, painters and any other thing that is positive.

And last, to my father Robert and all the men who have helped raise me, thank you! It's as simple as that. Happy Father's Day to you all!

Jun 17, 2018

*****

Part 3

The Other Inspirational Stuff

Now that you have read the remaining thoughts and the blogs I have written to date, I want to take you down another random path I tend to venture. For those that do not know, I love to take pictures of sunrises, sunsets, eagles and other birds and, well, anything I find interesting. The world fascinates me. Every now and again a picture I take will spark a thought or a message to share. This section is about those times where I share pictures with a message on social media or privately with friends. As I think of it I can find no better way to wrap up the 3 parts of this book than with truly inspirational messages and pictures from my cell phone. Some of these posts won't have pictures attached because I got them off the internet and weren't taken by me. I don't want to steal anyone else's hard work for my book. Without further ado, I ask that you take a trip with me.

*****

May Sunday find you in a place where you can appreciate all of the amazing gifts you have in your life. Perspective is the key!

*****

As a father I always want to be the guy with advice. To share wisdom and life lessons from a life well lived. If I had a daughter I would have shared simple beauty of the world. I don't, so for Father's Day I'll share it with you, my female friends. Find peace. Be peace. Give peace.
(Original message shared with video of the waves)

Do not be so consumed with the destination that you overlook the joys of the journey. Not all things in the rearview are bad. Life is about the yesterday, the today and the tomorrow. Find beauty, peace and inspiration in them all. The successes and failures of yesterday, the hands-on of making it happen today, and the endless possibilities of tomorrow.

(Original message shared with video)

*****

The truest lesson of life I could ever tell,

Is live life with your heart and live it well,

Speak words that ring true to you deep in your soul,

Life is full of adventure so get out and hit the road.

Someday you may not wake to see the cloudy day. So, before you complain about the day, the weather, being tired, jobs, money or even of aches and pains, think your eyes opened and today is yours. Honor it by honoring you and your gifts. Good morning, friends!

*****

It takes but a second to find something to take you away!

*****

I woke up and walked out my house down the road. I stood in front of people's houses and enjoyed the sunrise over their yards. I did not fear persecution or being shot. I did not worry that I shouldn't be out in this neighborhood. I simply walked and enjoyed. On this day of celebrating MLK I remind you and myself that although we have a long way to go, we have in fact come a long way. Have an amazing day, my friends.

*****

As I snapped pictures of dew drops something caught my eye,
Inside the leaves there was a bee that had died,
I sent this picture to a friend and sadly replied,
After seeing the bee she said "Oh no, poor guy",
But for me it was beauty I saw in this little bee,
In the background of raindrop picture it reminded me,
that we all face an end one day our breath will cease to be,

And in that death we shall leave a lifetime of stories,
and when it comes will someone see a life that's true?
Let it reflect your beliefs, your heart and all that matters to you!
(May you find peace in all your ventures today.)

The world is one breath away from being amazing. Your breath is the one we need. How will you use it to make someone's day? I share this with mine.

*****

We do not need to escape from our lives as many like to say,

We only need to be reminded that it is in us to make a way,

A way to a better day, a laugh and a smile,

Which can easily be found if we sit just a little while.

(Original message shared with video)

*****

Life is an adventure that will one day stop. Nothing we do, have done or wish to do will matter at that point. So why not enjoy the journey while we can?

*****

So much peace to be found,

in the moments we slow down,

As the trumpet plays across the sea,

I'm thankful for all the things I get to be!

May you find moments of peace. I share mine with you.

(Original message shared with video)

*****

Happy Mother's Day to you. I don't know if you are a good mom or bad. If you are a nurturer or not. I do know that it isn't easy being a parent. I know that you have made tough choices for your kid(s) and want to give them all you can. This morning I found these 2 cups on a rail and thought it was perfect. From a son and a father, I say, Happiest of Mother's Day.

When the night stretches its wings to take over the sky, The day slowly fades to sleep bidding us all goodbye. May you find the love in the day. Here is my gift of love for you. Smile bright, friends.

*****

At the heart of everything is a light that burns intensely. It is the energy that fuels us. It is the source of our strength. It is the essence of us. May you know yours intimately.

*****

Every minute of every day you have a chance to make your day better, make someone else's day better and make the world better. It doesn't take super acts to do it but rather small ones. Today, I start mine by sharing a bit of serenity from my journey. How will you make yours, someone else's or the world a little better today?
(Original message shared with video)

*****

In the darkness learn to find peace.

*****

Stopped in traffic. Looked up and saw this little love note.
I share with my friends.

*****

We have every choice in the world to engage in amazing. It doesn't take work to do, just a willingness to turn off the negative and appreciate the magic in the world. Happy Tuesday from my morning view, friends. Hope you share your own magic today!

*****

One day we will learn that a good day is simply the approach we take to it. May you take control of your day and make it amazing. TGIF friends!

*****

Tried to make a collage of sunrise/sunset pics I have my phone gallery. So hard to do but I came up with this. Now sharing it with my friends.

*****

It is easy to find a place to pause and see beauty. The hard part is knowing one can pause and do so.

*****

In the writer's hand resides the story he or she sees. In the singer's heart fuels the soul of the song that he or she sings. In the painter's brush the fire of the image waits to be unleashed. In the photographer's eye the picture is captured before the shutter clicks.

Art is perception. It is purposed by the writer, singer, painter and photographer. Yet, it is given meaning by the observer whose history plays the biggest part. Today I give four pictures turned into a collage because one thing can always be more if you look close enough.

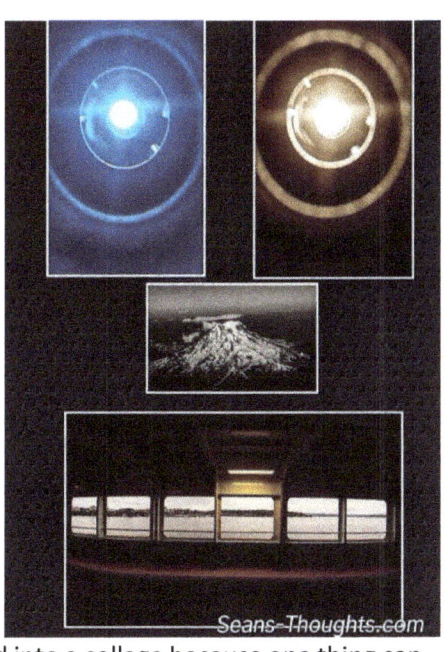

*****

In the end, where one is going is about anticipation,

excitement and exploring the unknown.
As it goes, no matter where one winds up, there will never be a place like the one called home.

*****

No matter how straight the path is, how pretty the world is or how excited we may be to take it, sometimes we just know the shit is coming. Every

journey has its negatives...walk it anyway because you never know if what looks bad could turn out great. For what it's worth, the seagulls fly away when you get near.

*****

The sun will set no matter what we do. The clock will continue to tick no matter how much time we try to save. Life will no longer be ours no matter how long we hope to gain another few moments. Embrace the moments life provides because there isn't a guaranteed tomorrow.

*****

A picture is worth 1000 words so it is said. A picture with two pictures, however, is not worth 2000 words no matter how stunning each picture is to the eye. Do not treat life this way. Every picture is worth its 1000 words just like each person is worth his or her value no matter what is also there. What is your picture of you worth?

*****

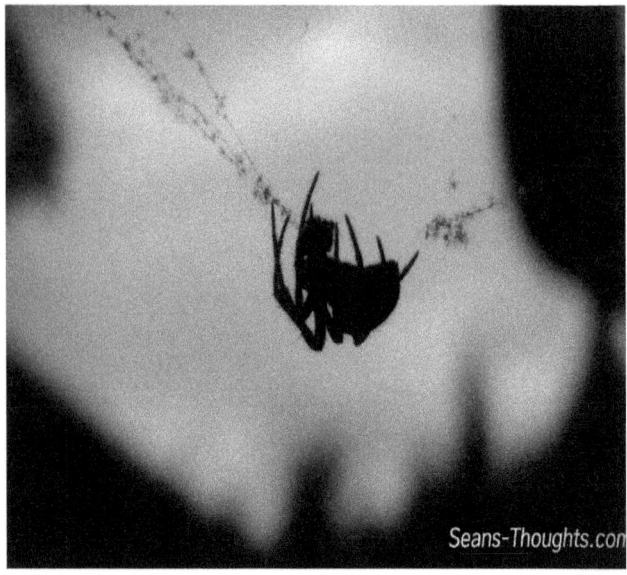

The spider does not care that one fears its eight legs,
It feels no remorse for the insects that get caught in its webs,
It simply lives for the moment that its prey finds its nest,
Savoring every morsel until fate snags the prey that's next,
The day will come when the spider's web will no longer be spun,
As it gives way to the next spider whose adventure have just begun.

*****

One does not need to go somewhere to be taken somewhere. Every view that we take has the potential to amaze. This morning I chased dewdrops on the flowers in my front yard. This collage is to remind you that life is a choice. Choose beauty. Choose smiles. Choose love. Most of all, choose yourself.

*****

Do not worry when the path gets cloudy, foggy or even just a little misty because the guiding light will always find a way through if you believe in your journey. Find the light even in the darkest times.

*****

Life is about perspectives. Each of us has the ability to see the same image but from vastly different points of view. Be open to seeing things in new ways.

*****

To be strong, one must be willing to stand up alone and shine one's light no matter how dark the horizon may be. Sometimes the light leading the way is the one you carry yourself. Stand tall and believe in you.

*****

The smallest of things can have a fierce impact on your world. Do not dismiss something or someone because it or he or she seems little to you. Some of the greatest moments of life are found just on the other side of judgement.

*****

Today I saw an angel on my drive,

I looked and there it was in the sky,

Even though I'm not religious I smiled at the view,

Because angel or not, I can share my moment with you,

So here is my moment captured by me,

I saw an angel... Now what do you see?

*****

Life is not horrible, ugly, vile or any of the things we like to attribute to it. It is not perfect, magical, inspiring or any of those things either. Life is perspective. It is what

you search for and what you seek to fill you up. It is your boat out on the water heading to wherever you want to go. Where are you heading?

*****

When you look up you will often find something that can amaze you. Here the owl visited my birdfeeder looking for dinner which he caught.

*****

Truth of life is as simple as this…. The stairs of life go both up and down. Some days we cannot control which way we are going but we always can control how we go about it. Enjoy the ride!

*****

Outside my door the eagle sat to rest,

The crows didn't want him near the nest,

So squawk and cackle they did attack,

Until the eagle flew away they hope he doesn't come back.

Look up, friends. There is more to the world than what is on our phones.

*****

Not every sunrise is bright and welcoming to the new day. Sometimes it is ominous in its mystery. Every moment can have its remarkable beauty providing we look for it. Open your eyes to the possibilities.

*****

Many don't realize that the difference in what they believe is a matter of perspective. We can all see the same thing yet paint a completely different picture. If we listen to each other, we may learn we are looking at the same thing.

*****

I arrived at the beach to enjoy the sunset. A father was with his son showing the kid how to fish. As I was leaving the boy as alone casting his line. I snapped a few pictures of this simple act. I walked down and  showed the father the pics I had taken and asked if he would like them. I texted them and left. Find moments of peace every day and your outlook on life will change for the better. I share this one with you.

*****

I know not where I am going but I go without a care,

Because this place or that place is on the way there,

In this place I might find you and that place I'll find someone new,

And along the way I'll smile because meeting new people is what I like to do.

*****

The past will always be that which we leave,

Fading into the distance of who we use to be,

Never forget the history and story of your days,

As you create the new memories as your future plays,

So live in the present and hold on tight,

Because life is short; enjoy the flight.

(Original message shared with video)

*****

When we see something stunning we often wish we were there. We actually envy the person who experienced it. Truth is we can have adventure wherever we are. It is our choice. This collage is 9 pictures taken over the past 3 days here in Port Orchard, Washington. An eagle, owl, sunrise and sunset pictures, flowers and even coffee cups holding the sun. Make life amazing. It is completely up to you. Enjoy my 3-day snapshot.

*****

It takes very little to see the magic in the world. Start looking for the things to make you smile, think and glow. When you do, you'll start seeing it everywhere. Light your own way.

*****

Life reflects what is given to it. It is a mirror taking in our energy and showing us what we are. Chase the sun, find the rays of light, steal the flickers in the stars and live fully. You never know what you'll find. I cleaned up this photo but it is real and it is mine. What have you been missing?

*****

There are many roads and paths that will appear in a lifetime. Some will be clear and easy to take. Others will be difficult. Whichever road you take make sure you stop and enjoy the journey because life is too short to simply worry about the final destination.

*****

The tree never told the mountains how magnificent they were, the mountains never told the setting sun its golden light shone amazingly across the sky, and the sunset never told the trees how regal they were touching the sky and the earth. Yet none of them were sad because each knew one special truth. That the others, though amazing, could never do what the other could do.

Be strong in the person you are because no one can do you better the person that is you.

*****

When the world gets too big and overwhelming, take a moment to slow down and see what is going on around you. This single raindrop is nothing to a person by itself, yet to the leaf it sits on, it is everything. To the ants, birds and small creatures, it can be life. One drop. Life is a gift. Take time to recognize what you have in it.

*****

This bird does not care that I pulled my truck over on the side of the road. This bird did not flinch as I angled to snap this picture. It simply exists in harmony with the world it lives in. We, as people, could learn a great deal from nature.

*****

Magnificence exists simply because it does. There is no need to search it out. Simply open your eyes and take in what you see.

*****

A city in the rearview as the ferry churns away,
A space needle stands tall boldly on display,
And a supermoon hiding just behind the city lights,
As the nocturnal of the species awaken for the night,
Dear Seattle, I'll return when the time has set me free,
Until then my photo of you will be my special memory!

*****

I could literally add more photos and more little captions to this part of the book but in the end, I wanted to stop at leaving Seattle. Why? We are always leaving. We are always headed somewhere throughout every day of our lives. We look at it as a blessing if the past was hard or a curse if the past was good. The truth is the magnificence of where we came from, should be admired and revered as we head to where we are going. Speaking of going, it is time I took us to the closing of this book. Nice segue right?

*****

CLOSING #1

I am not even sure how I got here to finishing round two of my author adventures. What I can say is that the responses I got from my first book told me a few things about my writing. First, I can reach people with just a thought. Second, my words open doors of conversation and give people things (of value) to talk about with each other. Lastly, many of the people I have gotten to talk to have a need to tell and share their respective stories with others. That is why book two exists: because the first opened so many minds and possibilities. I sincerely hope that book two has done the same.

Before I go on with my closing comments I have to once again thank my good friend April for all the work she has done on both book one and now book two. Every time I write something she takes a journey both in my world and within her own. I am forever grateful that she has chosen to join me on this ride. I could talk about her part in this but that would not be any fun. Instead, like in book one, I'll give April a chance to have her own closing remarks. For the record, and now on the record, last book I gave her a paragraph and she wrote four pages. I have no idea what she will write this time. I'll be back to close out this book after her message.

*****

APRIL'S MESSAGE

So here we are. The second book. Putting together the first book was such an amazing experience. I have used that word "amazing" a lot over the last year. So, what does that mean? Amazing. To look at something and just be in awe of what it is. I am in awe. We started this journey with a chance meeting. It became a question. It turned into an answer. That turned into a book. That's not where it stopped though. I believe this experience has been so much more than putting out a book. It was about connecting with people. Isn't that what the first book was about? Where this hit home for me most is in two stories, two very personal stories I've told the many, many people we've met along this journey.

One is about my mother. When we published the first book I sent my mother a copy. I was proud. I wanted her to see it. Yes, like any kid of any age, I wanted my mom to be proud too. What no one knows, including Sean, is that I sent it to her because I felt my mom needed it. While walking through each passage of the first book with Sean, I thought about my mom a lot. I was never really close to my mom. Don't misunderstand; I love her very much. But I held her at a distance and created an image of her as a weak and passive woman. I lived my life trying not to be those things. However, recently, I really wanted to connect with her. I wanted to understand her. I wanted to help her through some of the pain I believed she felt. Our work on the first book helped me to see how powerfully fulfilling genuine human connection can be. Up to that point, my mom and I just didn't have the words to talk, nor an idea where to begin. And, frankly, I wasn't sure even Sean's work could change that. I sent her a copy any way.

A few weeks later she called me, out of the blue, and told me that my friend made her cry. For the record, my mom lives in Las Vegas and I live in the Pacific Northwest and hadn't lived in Vegas for decades. I wasn't quite sure what friend she was referring to. She said, "Sean." I said, "Oh." I knew what she meant. She *did* read the book.

We talked for a while that day, and nearly every Sunday for weeks after. Those first few calls on Sunday afternoons were intense. We didn't just talk about the passages. Hell, we didn't really talk about them much after the first few calls. Instead, we talked about *her*. And one day, I know we'll talk about *us*. In part, because of that book, I understand my mom a little bit better. I understand she made some hard choices. She lived with consequences. Most were selfless. Some, selfish. But that's okay. She's human and I love her for it. For my mom and I, the book opened a door. We chose to walk in.

The second story is about a group of students, the same students Sean mentions in the second part of this book. At the beginning of the school year, I was asked to help develop a new course for students labeled as "reluctant". The main objective of the course was to help these students develop reading and writing skills so they could pass the standardized test required for graduation. I was given a lot of freedom to choose how and what I was going to teach to meet that objective. I went into teaching to share what I loved with my students: thinking, discussing, reading, writing ideas. Yes, ideas! (Thank you, Mrs. Roberta Cartwright and Ms. Erica Turner, wherever you are, for opening the door and inviting me in.) To say I was excited about designing this course would be an understatement.

But where to begin? Normally, I'd pull out high interest literature, current affairs articles, blog posts, etc. to keep their interest and get them reading, thinking, talking, writing. This time, though, I started with them. I asked them. Now, before some of you look alarmed at this choice, I want you to know that I love what I do, and at the risk of sounding arrogant, I am pretty good at it. What I wanted to know was what texts were going to get these students, in jeopardy of not completing high school, who were self-proclaimed non-readers and non-writers, to "buy what I was selling"? If I learned anything from my love of language and rhetoric, it is to "know your audience." I needed to get to know them. So, I did.

I realized from our first conversation that these young people thought deeply about their world, had strong beliefs and opinions, and, though their delivery of these ideas would make an English teacher cringe, they could articulate them thoughtfully.

The test was a momentary thing. They cared about the test to the extent that it would help them graduate. They wanted something real. They wanted something they could sink their teeth into. They wanted something else.

I realized the thing they were asking for was in the palm of my hand: Sean's book. Why not? My students had questions about life. They had ideas about life. They wanted to talk about life. My belief was, and still is, that the first book is just that: the springboard to discussing things that matter to us. As they read the passages, and wrote about them, they let down their defensive guards, they took risks with their writing, they connected with each other. They talked, they argued, they laughed, they cried. I strongly believe they began to feel they belonged at the table, that what they thought mattered.

I have learned several other lessons since Sean and I started working together. You have to be true to your own voice. When you're not, people know. I learned, as we talked to (and hugged) hundreds of people, that what is sadly missing from society today is the one thing we need most: human contact. We don't hug each other enough. We don't pat each other on the back enough. We don't say hello enough. People, we have to make the human connection. We would be much happier if we did.

I learned we don't know how much we don't know. The minute we pretend that we know everything is the moment we lose the opportunity to know so much more.

Anything that really matters is worth the hard work. The payoff may not come immediately and it isn't going to come in dollars. If you're chasing the dollars, you are crazy. There's got to be something more, something intrinsic that really matters to you. As we continue along this journey, hearing people's stories, connecting with people, I found the thing that matters to me. Find the thing for you.

I learned, too, we're all human. We make mistakes. We make choices. We live with the consequences. But all of us are human. Accept that in others. And accept it in yourself.

I'm excited to see where this goes. The second book. I was excited to see the evolution of writing and thought. The evolution of writing, well, that comes from the nerdy writing teacher in me. The evolution of thought, that's from the human in me. And, as I strongly believe, the evolution of how this book will affect people. Including people I care about.

Sean and I had a conversation the other night about whether or not he truly understood the impact he had on people. I believe that with the first book we only scratched the surface. I think this book will go deeper. I think the seeds of impact have been planted. I'm excited to see them grow. How? I don't know. When? I don't know that either. What I don't question is if? That I know. I've already seen it. If you're reading this book, you know too.

*****

CLOSING #2

As expected April had a few things to say, didn't she? That is what I appreciate about what we have done so far on this adventure, the passion of those we interact with including ourselves. I have to confess that I am scared to write a third book because I am not sure how many pages April will write if given another chance. All joking aside, I appreciate what she has done, said and shared. Now to close this out for real.

As I read part one of this book I realized how much turmoil our nation was in and is still in as I write this now. (July 2018 for the record). I am proud to be able to have shared a snapshot of the times and have others read it. Maybe it will spark better conversations between people. Maybe it will show us as human beings that the pain we feel is self-inflicted and repairable. Maybe it will bridge some gaps. I sure hope so.

Reading part two reminded me of how far I had come as a writer and how much I enjoy layering stories. While part three showed me the beauty that we can easily find in this world. I hope both inspires you, the reader, to find you own voice, words and beauty. It is a wonderful life. Enjoy it.

Last point, I know that my thoughts are not the perfect answer or the end all to be all but more a starting point for a conversation and understanding. As I read and edited each of these passages, messages, quips and stories I was transported to the thousands of conversations that stemmed from them.

This is part of my life. This is part of my soul and the very being that I am, not because I bare it in its entirety but more because I dare to challenge you to have your own thoughts and share them with the world. We need more of that in this world people who share their joys not their hate. People who want to learn about those who are different and want to grow from it.

So, share the message in your heart, not the hate. More importantly, share your joy. That is what I will close with. Share your joy, your story and a nice cup of coffee.

The next book of thoughts just might be yours. Until next time, friends...

www.ingramcontent.com/pod-product-compliance
Lightning Source LLC
Chambersburg PA
CBHW061214070526
44584CB00029B/3832